THE INCREDIBLE LIFE STORY OF SISTER ELENA AIELLO

THE

Incredible Life Story

OF

Sister Elena Aiello

The Calabrian Holy Nun
(1895 ~ 1961)

by
RT. REV. FRANCESCO' SPADAFORA
and translated from the Italianby
RT. REV. ANGELO R. CIOFFI'

ISBN: 978-93-5128-923-4(HB)

First Published in 1964
Indian Reprint in 2017
Published by

Kalpaz Publications
C-30, Satyawati Nagar,
Delhi – 110052
E-mail: kalpaz@hotmail.com
Website: kalpazpublications.com
Ph.: +91-9212142040

Cataloging in Publication Data—DK
Courtesy: D.K. Agencies (P) Ltd. <docinfo@dkagencies.com>

Spadafora, Francesco, author.
The incredible life story of Sister Elena Aiello : the Calabrian holy nun (1895-1961) / by Rt. Rev. Francesco Spadafora ; and translated from the Italian by Rt. Rev. Angelo R. Cioffi.
pages cm
Reprint. Originally published: Brooklyn, N.Y. : Theo. Gaus' Sons, 1964.
ISBN 9789351289234 (HB)

1. Aiello, Elena, 1895-1961. 2. Blessed—Italy—Biography. 3. Suore Minime della Passione di Nostro Signore Gesù Cristo—Biography. 4. Nuns—Italy—Biography. I. Cioffi, Angelo R., translator. II. Title.

BX4537.7.Z8A85 2017 DDC 282.092 23

DECLARATION

In conformity with the Decree of Pope Urban VIII, the Author declares his intention to attach purely human credibility to events narrated in this book. He nowise presumes to anticipate the judgment of Holy Mother Church.

CONTENTS

Introduction

THREE IMPORTANT DEPOSITIONS were made at the time of Sister Elena's death: one at the time of her funeral at Cosenza, the second and third on the tenth and thirtieth day of her demise.

The first one is by Father Francis Sarago of the Minims—a learned and venerable Religious who was Sister Aiello's spiritual director for many years and well-known to the younger clergy of Calabria.

Here it is:

"There is always something to learn while facing a coffin. We behold the mystery of time and eternity, the poverty and richness of life, the mystery of the human body, which turns into dust, and of the spirit that hails from God and returns to Him. These thoughts hold good at the time of a funeral, but, more so, for many people who have a contemplative mind.

However, not all the pilgrims who are travelling from time to eternity behave in the same manner when fulfilling their duties and expressing their love for God and neighbor.

Hence, if the heroes, the genii, are the honor of mankind, far more so are the saints, the living images of God, who enlighten the world by their charity. For it is through charity that true greatness is achieved. If great minds and hearts hold a special place in history, so does this departed one in whose presence we now are. Let us briefly recollect our thoughts on this subject in order that we may understand the overall plan, may thank God for it, and also benefit by its timely lessons.

We may consider the life of Sister Elena Aiello under three vital aspects: i.e.

(1) As the Foundress of the Minim Tertiaries of the Passion of Our Lord Jesus Christ.
(2) As a contemplative soul.
(3) As a martyr to suffering.

1. THE FOUNDRESS was born at Montalto Uffugo on April 10, 1895. After a short time in the Congregation of Sangue Sparso in Nocera, she was compelled to return home on account of illness. There, after a miraculous recovery, she disclosed to her friend, Sister Gigia Mazza, her intention to establish a Religious Community. Taking the great wonder worker of Paola as their guide, they adopted "Charity" as their banner. It was thus that the Institute started on January 17, 1928, winning recognition on January 20, 1948, and the official approval on July 1949.

The Community's special object is to practice charitable works, specifically to provide a home for orphan girls. The Nuns aim at protecting in every way little girls whether orphaned or just abandoned. Besides giving them a solid christian education, they teach them housekeeping, sewing, embroidering, etc., and thus they afford them the opportunity to earn an honest livelihood and to become a pattern for good both to society and to family as well.

Furthermore, the Sisters do catechetical work, prepare late candidates for First Communion and Confirmation and occasionally they do housekeeping for the Seminary, if requested by the Bishop of the Diocese. They also take care of old and invalid Priests in suitable homes.

Thus the Kingdom of Christ becomes actual reality through the beautiful virtue of charity which is merciful love, love for those who need spiritual food for the soul as well as bread for the body—the love taught by Jesus Who was ever doing good, converting sinners, consoling the afflicted and healing the sick.

True love is concerned with human suffering and is anxious to relieve it as much as possible in imitation of the Good Samaritan, who alights from his horse to dress up and heal the wounds of humanity.

Sister Elena Aiello was quick to perceive that there was a great number of abandoned girls. She went looking for them, and having found them, she took care of them.

Her compassionate heart led her to provide loving mothers for so many girls and with indomitable will, she kept on fostering her charitable works.

Like all works blessed by God, the Tertiary Minims of the Passion are ever expanding and strengthening their charitable activities.

Just now they conduct a Novitiate, an Orphanage and some catechetical courses at Cosenza, a Teachers' Training and the "Istituto Magistrale Parificato" a Boarding School at Montalto Uffugo: also an Orphanage and a Boarding School in a nearby section, and still another Orphanage, Grammar Schools and Kindergarten at Paola.

Similar institutions are located at Marano Marchesato, Cerchiara, Bucita, and San Vito di Cosenza. At San Lucio there is a Home for the Aged, and catechetical programs are functioning in Rome, Orsomarso, San Sisto, San Fili, Castrovillari, Carolei, Rovito, Spezzano Piccolo and Lauropoli.

In order to look after the establishment and the proper management of her houses, Sister Elena, though bedridden, was ever watching and praying that God would abundantly bless, keep and prosper her institution.

2. THE CONTEMPLATIVE SOUL — Unfortunately, nowadays people don't pray much; hence, they lead a life that is poor both spiritually and socially. To lead a full life, we must turn to our Heavenly Father so that by contemplating His Majesty and love, we instinctively beseech Him for life and strength to persevere in the fulfilment of our duties to the very end of our days, with a confident expectation of our eternal reward.

According to St. Augustine the essence of our Holy Religion consists precisely in that mode of prayer. And that was the prayer of Sister Elena Aiello whose soul was constantly united to her God. She prayed not only for her own needs, for the needs of her Institution, of the orphan girls and of all those soliciting her help, but she prayed as well for the whole world, as a true christian soul should.

People were so sure of it that they frequently called on her, on her Nuns or on the Orphans, whenever they were in need of spiritual or temporal help. Sister took care to stress the importance of prayer in the Holy Rule. By her insistence on prayer she deserved to be praised, both by individuals and by society: for only the love of God and of our neighbor constitutes true greatness.

3. A MARTYR TO SUFFERING — Generally speaking, the world does not appreciate the value of suffering. St. Bonaventure says that there are three logical steps in our lives: birth, death, rebirth—and that the second one is the most important of them: for it is only through suffering that we may hope for our rebirth in heaven. The grain of wheat will not yield its fruit unless it is first buried into the ground. The mystery of Redemption was accomplished on the Cross "When I shall be lifted up, I shall draw all things to Myself." Thus Jesus spoke. We must imitate Him. It is through humiliation and abasement that we achieve admission to His Father's House. Only those who are nailed to the Cross with the Crucified will be able to save the world. One day Jesus said to Gemma, "I need victims, but, oh! real sterling victims!"

Who could adequately measure the sufferings endured by this great departed soul? She suffered martyrdom in her body, where every single fibre was tortured. She was unable to take food, unable to move about, and was worn out by fever during her last years. Besides, she suffered severe and painful hemorrhages that undermined her strength until the bell of departure tolled for her.

But by far, more bitter were the tortures of her soul, because she intensely bewailed the evils afflicting the world. She was ever worrying over the welfare of souls, and over the exact discipline of monastic life. Hers was the agony of the victim freely consecrated to Jesus agonizing in the Garden—a truly perfect martyrdom and consequently a real redemptive work.

Sister Elena pleads with us not to ignore the spiritual and temporal ills of the world. Since we are the children of the same Heavenly Father we ought to share with one another both sorrows and joys and thus show that we are members of one big family.

She summons us to pray, for prayer is the breath of the soul. When we pray, we feel united by a common bond, we are reminded that we are going together on a journey that leads us to the same destination, i.e., to our ultimate reunion in our Father's House. She wants us to uphold the rights of justice against the arrogance of might, to do away with the old man and replace him with the new one, the man of light and liberty. God's children are only those who crucify their flesh with its vices and concupiscences.

She raises her voice to tell us that her charitable institutions must not end in failure but rather, by daily improvement, to become a source of great blessings in all parts of the world. Every mother lives in her children and so does Mother Elena live in her daughters. Her Institute is a light that must not go out, but rather, move forward from its original place, from this Calabrian land, from this great soul of our Cosenza."

✝ ✝ ✝

THE SECOND DEPOSITION. — On June 29, 1961, Father Bonaventura da Pavullo, member of the Superior Council of the Capuchins and Pontifical Assistant to the Sister Minims of the Passion, wrote to Mother Vicar Sister Gigia Mazza, as follows:
"Very Reverend Mother and dear Sisters in Jesus and Mary:

It's now the tenth day since your beloved Mother passed away. She went to heaven, at dawn . . . when persons and things are at rest. Her cherished desire was fulfilled when two Priests and a multitude of heavenly spirits came to assist her and make easier her passage to eternity. Her soul went to meet her Divine Spouse, at the very time of the Resurrection, holding in her hand the oil-filled and brightly burning lamp.

As the Priests were ascending the Altar for the renewal of the Holy Sacrifice of Calvary, she too was bringing to an end her long martyrdom, in intimate union with the Divine Victim, with the Most Holy Crucified One. For she had consecrated herself to Him from earliest childhood with a bond of tender love and had remained faithful to the very end. Her last word: "Fiat"—"Be it done"—"Consummatum est"—"It is consumated!"

She has taken her flight to eternity from this "Eternal City" so dear to her, because it is the dwelling place of the "dolce Cristo in terra," as she loved to say with St. Catherine when mentioning the Holy Father. Rome had a peculiar appeal to her heart: it was eminently the Holy City on account of the glorious tombs of the Princes of the Apostles so jealously preserved there.

Here, in Rome, she was blessed with the friendship of many a devoted person, of special benefactors of her Institute and other charitable works. So it pleased Divine Providence that, before going to her eternal rest, she would have to be here in order, as it were, to thank them and assure them of her boundless gratitude. For friendship and gratitude were something very sacred to Sister Elena.

And now orphaned you are, dear Sisters!

The one who was like a father and mother for you—loving, yet firm—is gone forever. Once she found out God's Will concerning her, she labored unceasingly to establish a new Religious Community based on a spirit of love and made secure by good discipline.

Since you were of one mind with her, you eagerly followed her on the hard road to perfection to which she invited you more by her deeds than by words. There was a bond of supernatural love between her heart and yours, between her motherly spirit and yours so utterly devoted to her.

You know she loved you without any preference, because she loved you in God alone, and loved her Institute better than her own life. No amount of harships, humiliations, struggles, would deter her from her resolve to uphold, to enlarge, defend and render it more efficient before God and men.

She made sure above all that her Institute would fully realize the great charitable mission which God had assigned to it. We heard her saying more than once: "Even from my tomb I shall raise my voice against anyone daring to oppose the charitable goal of my Community."

So, after all, you are not really orphans, dear Sister Minims of the Passion. For, as a matter of fact, your Mother General is still living in the midst of you.

She lives because of the Holy Rule and of the other regulations she gave you.

She lives because of the untold sufferings she endured with perfect resignation in her humble cell.

She lives above all, because of her loving protection for all of you from the heavenly abode so richly earned by her burning love for Jesus and Mary and by the exercise of the finest christian virtues.

Now it is up to you in a special way, and also up to those who esteemed her in life, to hasten, by prayers and good works, the day of the infallible judgment by Holy Mother Church. Amen.

✝ ✝ ✝

These two convincing depositions portraying the essential aspects of the life and work of Sister Elena Aiello, have been our guide in the presentation of her biography.

On July 20, 1961, "L'OSSERVATORE ROMANO" printed our announcement on the thirtieth day of Sister Elena's death. "On the 19th of this past June, the busy life of Sister Elena Aiello came to an end in the Community House on Baldassini Street. She was born on April 10, 1895, at Montalto Uffugo (Cosenza)."

On January 28, 1928, together with the Mother Vicar—later on Mother General—she started the project to which she was to dedicate all her life. She began by gathering little abandoned girls in order to give them proper support and a good christian education.

She chose the Passion of Our Lord and the charity of St. Francis of Paola, as the leading guide of her Community, which she named: "Sister Minims of the Passion of Our Lord Jesus Christ." She leaves after her eighteen Houses, all in excellent condition and located in three Dioceses: i.e., Cosenza, Cassano, Roma and about 150 Sisters. On February 1948, the Sacred Congregation of the Religious gave formal approval to the Community of that zealous Calabrian Nun.

"The just man does indeed pass away, but his light remains:

the roadbed of charity, as planned by Sister Elena Aiello, not only holds fast, but it is even destined to get stronger and to move forward. The light of her charity shall ever brighten the path of her Community. Who can possibly forget her outstanding personality, her constant sufferings and the wilful opposition she met from quarters that aimed to crush and humiliate her young Community?"

"Though mostly bedridden for nearly twenty years, she ever kept praying and working from her small room. Suffering was her normal way of life. Nevertheless, she always welcomed and greeted those who needed her with a sweet smile. She felt keenly the pain, the anxiety and the tribulations of all who came to her, and with them she suffered, and for them she prayed. Suffering, if well accepted, is a gift of the Holy Spirit, a source of supernatural joy and the distinctive trait of the Christian. It is really the sublime paradox of Christianity, a mark of predilection which, owing to the charity shown to the little ones and to the afflicted, leads the way to that simple faith which is all powerful with God.

"She prayed for those who never pray, and offered up all her sufferings for the world's loose morals. She frequently spoke about Rome and the Holy Father for whom she had special veneration and love. And she offered herself as a victim to God for the welfare of the Pope and of Holy Church.

"On several occasions, she mentioned quite clearly her approaching end. For a period of two months she was subject to a persistent high fever that was resistant to medical care, though the diagnosis proved consistently negative. Nevertheless she decided to come to Rome on June 8, for in Rome she had desired to finish her painful journey. Her mortal remains have been returned to her beloved Calabria and are now resting at the Mother House in Cosenza."

The above quoted depositions have dealt with our subject in an inverse order, i.e., from the time of Sister Elena's death to the time of her birth. We shall now follow the other way round with the aid of some note books containing precious information from her birth to 1937. We shall also avail ourselves of the qualified statements by Monsignor Gaetano Mauro, Dean of Montalto, confessor and spiritual director of young Elena, as well as by statements of Sister Agatha Napoli, a co-postulant at Pagani and presently Superior of her Community "Sangue Sparso" in the St. Pius X Rest Home in Rome.

Besides a first hand account by the late Mother General, who was closely associated with Sister Elena from 1923 on, there are other Nuns also and some of her closest relatives, now still living, who could give additional information on some other particular events.

An accurate biography could be written only under such conditions. In the work in which we are now engaged, we shall only put down, from 1935 onward, whatever we have actually seen or heard, as well as what we could gather from the considerable correspondence in our possession.

CHAPTER ONE

The Flowering of a Vocation

SISTER ELENA AIELLO was born at Montalto Uffugo (cosenza) on Holy Wednesday, April 10, 1895 at 10 A.M. She was the child of Pasquale Aiello and Teresa Paglilla, whose house was located at the corner of Mercato Street on the Enrico Bianco Square. According to several documents, including the identification card issued by the Cosenza City Hall, November 12, 1937, her birthday was April 16, and so it was generally believed. But the late counsellor Di Napoli, a fellow citizen, and a devoted friend of Sister Elena, was able to correct that date through research of the City Hall records. In fact, Easter Sunday of that year took place on April 14, and we know it was during Holy Week that Sister Elena was born, according to the statement of all the witnesses, and that, for that very reason, she received in Baptism the name of Santa after the names of Elena and Emily.

The fact of her birth was duly registered at City Hall on Monday, April 15. On the same day the baby was baptized by the Pastor, Father Francis Benincasa, in the Church of San Domenico, formerly a property of the Parish of Santa Maria Assunta della Serra. The godmother was Mrs. Mary Genise.

Elena, the baby's first name, had been expressly chosen by her mother for a special reason. According to her, during the Procession of the Rogations, she had prayed for the grace of a baby girl. If granted, she would name her Elena and consecrate her to the Cross of Our Lord in memory of the Empress, St. Elena.

The city of Montalto Uffugo, with its twelve thousand inhabitants, rises over lovely hills reaching an altitude of 475 meters. It enjoys a superb panorama and it overlooks the Crati Valley. Northward it is bound by the distant Pollino mountain range, eastward by the massive Sila Mountains, westward by the Apennines, and southward by the gorge, at the confluence of Busento and Crati, which is dominated by the Seven Hills adorning the City of Cosenza.

Little Elena was surely blessed with an exemplary, christian environment. Pasquale Aiello enjoyed the reputation of being one of the best tailors of that region, so much so that his cilentele extended even as far as Cosenza.

This is the way counsellor Di Napoli describes him: "He was a fine looking man, exceptionally honest, very polite, the type of the true gentleman; he respected everybody and he was likewise respected." His shop, which was on the ground floor of his house, was very busy on account of the steady work and of the many boys who were learning the trade. The upper floor was reserved for his family. Teresa Paglilla, his wife, died, still young, on December 1, 1905, leaving eight children: Emma, Ida, *Elena*, Evangelina, Elisa, Riccardo, Giovannina and Francesco. Another daughter, M. Theresa, had gone to heaven one month earlier, being only one year old. Emma, the oldest, was quite young when her mother died, and Francesco was only a few months old.

It was then that the sterling virtue of that humble tailor stood out in all its beauty. He forthwith summoned all his children home, because he wanted to look personally after their christian education. They all sought to help their father in his daily work, as well as they could, considering their age and occupations.

Good old Pasquale had far exceeded the proverbial age of eighty when he died, November 16, 1955, at Montalto, the very town where he was born, February 22, 1861. He had kept on working to the very end of his days, comforted by the loving care of Emma, his dear first born daughter.

Elena, the third child, was eleven years old, when her mother passed away. Only a few months earlier she had received the Sacrament of Confirmation from the Most Reverend Bishop Sorgente in the Chapel of Marchioness, Donna Amalia Spada.

Her godmother was Donna Agnesina Turano. Endowed with a bright mind, at the age of four she had already learned the principal elements of the Catechism, and, at the age of six she was sent to the Sisters of the Most Precious Blood to attend grammar school and to continue her religious instruction. While in that Institution, our little one, after morning prayers, would always attend Holy Mass, but, since the Holy Sacrifice was not offered daily there, little Elena, quietly eluding the Sister in charge, would quickly run to the nearby Church and thus satisfy her heart's desire. On one occasion it happened that, when running to Church, she fell on a piece of glass that cut her upper lip. Some people passing by took her home, and there the family doctor, Adolfo Turano, sealed the wound with a few stitches. After school time, as soon as she came home, she would spend the time sewing under her sister's supervision.

Very much pleased with her progress and her efforts to get a better understanding of the Catecsism, the Nuns used to take her along when she was hardly eight years old with the idea of preparing her to teach christian doctrine to the little ones. On June 21, 1904, Elena, at the age of nine, received First Holy Communion after careful preparation and a retreat preached by the Very Reverend Father Timoteo, a Passionist. Toward the end of the Retreat she went to Father Timoteo for confession together with many other girls and sought and got permission to wear the penitential belt.

After the Mission was over, our young lady called on her cousin Clara whose house adjoined the temporary residence of the Missionaries. One day while removing the wooden bar across the door, Clara unintentionally hit Elena on the mouth causing her to lose her two front teeth. Regardless of pain and a bleeding mouth, Elena put the teeth in the handkerchief and hurried to Father Timoteo for the promised penitential belt. Although her teeth had already undergone the process of mutation, new ones came through once more.

These few details give us an idea of the love of mortification and suffering, which clearly stands out all through future events, and they form, as it were, a striking pattern in the life of Sister Elena. With her, suffering was habitual, constant, and lovingly accepted. After her mother died, Elena, already an expert in the art of sewing, managed, together with her sisters, to assist her father in all his needs. Any of her free time was devoted to household duties, and, of course, to her usual daily prayers. Her first thought every morning was to attend Holy Mass and to receive Holy Communion. Not even a shadow of vanity or any worldly fashion ever entered the serene life of Pasquale Aiello's family.

The note-book goes on as follows: "On the Christmas Eve of 1906, Elena and Evangelina happened to observe an amusing incident from their house. While relating the story to their father, to distract him from the thought of their mother's passing on the previous year, it happened that Elena, while laughing, suffered a fit of convulsive coughing due to some water going through the windpipe while drinking.

The net result was that for a year and a half she underwent the lowering of her voice because of the steady coughing that stopped only at night. Medical care didn't help. At last Dr. Francesco Valentini of Cosenza prescribed an enema to flush the stomach. Since these repeated treatments were causing her intense pain, Elena, one evening, after saying the Rosary, as usual, made a promise to the Blessed Virgin of Pompei that she would become a Nun in that Church, if cured from that painful sickness.

In 1908, the Blessed Virgin of Pompei appeared to her in a vision during the night and assured her she would be healed. As a matter of fact, by morning, all symptoms of the disease had definitely disappeared, and so Elena gladly returned to the Marigliano Marini Institute under direction of the Sisters of the Most Precious Blood. Young Elena now had but one desire, i.e., the fulfillment of her promise to be a Nun at Pompei. The environment of a Sisters' Convent—that's what she was living for. However, she had to wait longer than she thought, for her wise father decided to postpone any decision on account of the local and foreign complications which led to the outbreak of the 1915 World War.

Calabria, besides mourning for the heroic deaths of her sons in the trenches and for the violent clashes on the battlefield, though badly shaken by the storm of the unparalleled national conflict, found strength enough to welcome refugees arriving from the Venetian region. She also sheltered a considerable number of Austrian prisoners on the Sila Mountains, although she herself was being harassed by the fury of the raging epidemic much more than the outlying areas on account of her poor sanitary conditions. In fact, "The Spagnola Flu" was playing havoc throughout whole districts and towns. Even Montalto did not escape the plague. However, it seemed that our young lady was getting incredible strength in the performance of extraordinary charity in spite of that contagion. Of course, she was fortunate to have, as a model of charity, that dynamic Sister Superior Angelica, and that zealous Priest, don Francesco Rizzo.

Elena used to spend the day nursing the poor invalids and even making up rough wooden caskets "for the christian burial" —as she used to say— of the plague victims.

During the time of the epidemic, Master Pasquale permitted Elena to spend the nights with the Sisters of the Institute for fear that she might communicate the disease to his family. So the Sisters began to consider her as one of their very own, and they even caressed the hope that someday she would become a member of their Community.

However, this young aspirant to religious life had chosen, long before, the right road to a life of charity. So to make sure of her vocation and of her spiritual perfection, she was caring for the poor, the sick, and the dying. Quite significant are the two episodes written with childlike simplicity in her copy books. One day Dr. Turano happened to find Elena combing bedridden Bianca C., whom everybody shunned because of her tubercular condition. Taking her by the ear, he led her back to her father saying: "My dear Pasquale, either you tie her to the bed, or I will do so, because she takes serious chances with no consideration to herself and with grave danger of catching the flu."

She used to hurry to the bedside of the dying especially of those who refused the Sacraments. One day having heard of the serious illness of Alessandro A., a freemason, she called on him and tried, ever so gently, to persuade him to receive the Sacraments. The answer was an emphatic "No!" But Elena kept on insisting so much that the sick man, in a fit of anger, grabbing a bottle, flung it at her. By lowering her head, Elena missed the blow to her face but was struck on the neck suffering a large wound as shown by the scar later on. Pressing the wound with a cloth, she hurried back to the sickbed, and in her sweet way she begged him again to receive the Sacraments because his soul was hanging on the edge of a precipice. She even told him she would not leave, unless he promised to welcome the Priest.

Such heroic charity deeply touched the sick man who readily promised to do so, but on one condition, i.e., that Elena would come and assist him every day. So he received the Sacraments from Father Eugenio Scotti and, for three months to the very day of his happy death, he received Elena's attention and care. Thus, through her charitable efforts, he became a fervent Christian bearing all his sufferings with patience and resignation.

So well-known was Elena's charitable activity that Father Ripoli, the chancellor of the Diocese, requested her to visit a man dying of cancer who was in great fear for having betrayed God. In fact, he had joined the Freemasons in order to provide for his children's future. Again Elena was able to appease him and had Father Leone, a Capuchin well-known to many of us at Cosenza, prepare him for the worthy reception of the Sacraments.

By her practice of charity and her desire to consecrate herself to God, we get a glimpse of Elena's consuming love for the Crucified, a love she had fostered since earliest childhood and which ended only with her death.

Elena was ready to fulfil whatever plans God had intended for her. "For a man's merits are not to be estimated by his having many visions or consolations, nor by his knowledge in Scriptures, nor by his being placed in a more elevated station, but by his seeking always purely and entirely the honor of God, by his esteeming himself as nothing and sincerely despising himself, and by being better pleased to be despised and humbled by others than to be the object of their esteem." (*Imitation of Christ*—Challoner translation—Book III, chapter 7 number 5.).

We shall presently see how the practice of charity remained constant with her, grew in intensity, and took hold of her very life. Even after her death that charity program has been expanding because of her projects of loving care for an ever growing number of orphan girls.

CHAPTER TWO

A Crude Operation Without Anesthetic

PASQUALE AIELLO, after mature consideration of Elena's firm decision, now that the post-war crisis was over, granted his permission on one condition, i.e., that she would enter the Institute directed by the Sisters of the Most Precious Blood. Hence, Elena left Montalto and went to Nocera dei Pagani in company with the Mother General, Sister Maria Co', on her very name day, August 18, 1920. She had previously visited Sister Teresa Vitari of the Capuchins in Cosenza, to seek the advice of one who enjoyed a saintly reputation. The good Sister explained to her the difficulties of the religious life. Elena replied that all she desired was Jesus Christ Crucified. Thereupon Sister Teresa advised her to join the Sisters of Divine Providence, who, only recently, had taken possession of the Cosenza Convent, where the saintly Vitari happened to be the sole resident member of the Capuchins.

However, she did not hesitate to tell her that she wouldn't last long with the Sisters of the Most Precious Blood, because God had other plans in store for her. Elena, after paying a short visit to her sister Giovannina, who was staying with Mrs. Luigina Garofalo during her school days, lost no time to give notice of her decision to Monsignor Angelo Sironi, Vicar of the Cosenza Archidiocese and her Spiritual Director for about one year. This prelate approved Elena's decision to go to the Mother House of the Sisters of the Most Precious Blood.

There, the young Calabrian was put in charge of sixteen postulants—an evident proof of the high esteem and confidence the Mother General reposed in her. That duty was fulfilled diligently and with unusual tact. Suffering took hold of her almost immediately and lasted for whole months. She was at first troubled with intestinal fever during one month, then on the first Sunday of October, while getting ready for the "Supplica" to our Lady of Pompei, she felt a severe pain on the left shoulder, right after shifting a heavy case together with one of the Nuns. After the "Supplica" the pain increased. Elena confided her trouble to Sister Emilia, with whom she had been acquainted from childhood at Montalto. Following Sister's advice she resolved to say nothing more. But her confessor, the venerable Father Villanacci, ordered her to reveal it to Mother Superior.

No further attention was paid to it until the month of March. One day, while Mother General was going upstairs, she happened to see, through a small window, Elena in a faint on the laundry floor. She was immediately picked up, and, under examination, it was found that her entire left shoulder up to the neck was a solid black mass. The physician, who had been summoned, ordered an operation. Still they tarried along, and all the while a persistent fever was raging on.

At last the Sisters decided to have the Community Doctor perform the operation for which they assumed all responsibility. On March 25th, (Holy Tuesday) Elena, sitting down and tied to a chair in her dormitory, bore the cutting of her blackened flesh without any kind of anesthetic. All the while she clutched a small wooden cross and kept gazing at a picture of Our Lady of Sorrows. Unfortunately, the physician cut off not only some flesh, but also some of the nerves, thereby causing a stiff shoulder and locked jaw. The ill-effect on the poor patient was terrible, especially the vomiting spell that tortured her for forty days.

As the time of the clothing ceremony was approaching, Elena, wishing to receive the religious habit, by sheer will-power, even though her wound was still open, got up from bed and followed all the Retreat exercises. To adjust the defective shoulder she tried to wear a corset that improved it somewhat. But, when Father Director saw Elena in such a deplorable condition, he couldn't let her go on. So he firmly insisted that she should return home until her complete recovery. Later on she could return to the Convent.

In her note-book Elena mentions that, at that very time, just a few days before leaving the Convent, Our Lord asked her, on two occasions, to accept His own designs with complete resignation and to embrace the Cross He had prepared for her! On May 2, 1921, Mother Superior notified Master Pasquale, by telegram, that Elena was returning home. But, before the telegram arrived, Master Pasquale heard someone knocking at the door, at four o'clock in the morning, and saying in a clear tone of voice: "Pasquale, Elena will be here tomorrow." Hurrying to the balcony above the door to see who had been knocking, Master Pasquale saw, coming down the staircase, a bent down and bearded old monk who was going towards the Church of St. Francis of Paola. Elena returned to Montalto on the 3rd of May, but, oh, in what a wretched condition.

The Mother General of the Sisters in Nocera had complimented Elena, as she was leaving, with these words: "My dear daughter, I should have been more than pleased if you had stayed with us just for the sake of praying in our Chapel: but the condition of your health necessarily demands that you return home. You have my fondest wishes for a prompt recovery and for your happy return to us." At the same time the Reverend Sisters had written to the Dean of Montalto, Monsignor Mauro, begging him not to say anything to the family about what had caused Elena's serious condition. Monsignor Mauro obliged, merely saying that Elena was sick. That was all. All the details concerning that operation without anesthetic were confirmed by Sister Agata Napoli, Elena's co-postulant at Pagani, and presently Superior of St. Pius X Rest Home at Rome (Via delle Spighe No. 1).

"Elena was so good-natured, so patient in suffering"—commented the good Sister. "The shifting of that case filled with linens . . . that incessant work . . . then that operation. She was clasping a wooden Crucifix she dearly loved. How she feared she would have to leave the Sisters! She was weeping while saying: "I weep because Mother wouldn't want to keep me here anymore." And when Mother decided to send her home, Elena, leaning against the work-room door, tearfully sighed: "See! Mother is sending me home!"

CHAPTER THREE

Who Snapped That Braid from Her Head?

ELENA HAD WASTED AWAY to such an extent that one would have hardly known her. She was unable to bathe and comb her hair. Her left arm was paralyzed and the purulent sore on the shoulder was about swarming with worms. Master Pasquale took her to Professor Roberto Falcone, Director of the City Hospital in Cosenza. There the patient told him everything.

The Doctor, after examining her, remarked: "Young lady, there is nothing I can do for you, because they have butchered you. The Doctor who performed your operation was not a surgeon: he cut the nerves. You may get your health back, but only by a miracle; in fact, the gangrene is already setting in!" Then turning to her father he advised him to demand compensation from that Institute. But Elena, stepping in, pleaded with her father to do nothing of the kind, the more so because she still hoped to return to Pagani and resume her religious life.

Thus she started that long and trying period of suffering in her little room at Montalto. Confined to her bed almost every day, she managed to walk to the Sisters' Institute once a week in order to go to confession. To hide her deformed figure, she would take a short cut through the garden adjoining the Institute. She received Holy Communion every Thursday. Those were the months of silent suffering, but ever brightened by the hope that some day she could be active again. During the month of August, 1921, her dream seemed to fade away after experiencing a sharp pain in her stomach. The liquid food, that was being forced with a small spoon through the corner of her mouth, was being rejected almost every hour.

The Doctors in charge prescribed an accurate examination and X-ray pictures. Hence, she was taken back to the City Hospital at Cosenza. There Dr. Cerrito, after examining the X-ray pictures, pronounced that there was cancer in her stomach. He explained the gravity of the disease to Giovannina, Elena's sister, and he clearly stated that, although Elena could have survived for some time even with her afflicted shoulder, now there was no hope on account of cancer. "I am sorry for her—he added—but there is no cure for cancer." He had hardly finished speaking when Elena, entering the room, in that frank way of hers, and with strong faith, turned to the physician saying: "My dear Doctor, it is you, who are going to die: I will not die from this disease, because St. Rita is going to make me well." One may easily imagine what little belief, if any, the good doctor put in that prediction of a recovery that was out of the question.

Elena, though very tired, instead of returning to Montalto at once, preferred to stop for a while at the home of her cousin Elvira Landolfi Aiello, in the neighborhood of San Gaetano's parish church. Before going into the house, Elena entered the Church and fervently beseeched St. Rita, whose statue was venerated there, to cure her of that stomach trouble. In her note-book she relates that, while praying, she beheld dazzling flames all around the statue. Turning to the cousin next to her, she told her, quite astonished, that the statue was burning. The cousin who had seen nothing, didn't understand what Elena really meant. That night, the Saint appeared to Elena telling her she wanted some devotional exercises to be held in her honor, at Montalto, in order to rekindle the faith of those people. She added further that a triduum should be held in her honor.

Returning to Montalto on the following day, Elena started the triduum to St. Rita, after which the vision took place again. The Saint instructed her to repeat it once more, after which she would recover from her stomach trouble. However, her sore shoulder would linger on because she had to suffer for the sins of the world. Once again she expressed a desire for devotional exercises in her honor at Montalto.

The reality of these visions and the truth of the above statements are also vouched for by Monsignor Mauro, who, at that time, was Elena's Confessor and Spiritual Director. That Prelate very kindly confirmed the above statement to us right here in Rome on October 20, 1963. His statement is exceedingly valuable. As a matter of fact, Elena was completely cured of that cancer condition on October 21st at 5 o'clock in the morning—a day so decisive in her life.

We read further in the note-book: "October 21, 5 o'clock in the morning, St. Rita of Cascia appeared to me in a vision from her little niche, radiant with light. After walking around the room she approached the bed and, folding the coverlet she placed her right hand on my stomach saying: "Now you may eat anything you desire, because you are cured. But I want that a new statue be placed in the Church of San Domenico and precisely in St. Joseph's niche." Here we should mention that the Church of San Domenico, which had been extensively damaged during the 1905 earthquake, was not frequented by Elena at the time. In fact, she didn't even know where St. Joseph's niche was located. Evangelina, her sister, who, from the adjoining room, had seen the brilliant light, filtering from Elena's room through the door cracks, suspecting fire, quickly got up and entered. Approaching the bed, she thought that Elena was unconscious. So, fearing she might be really dead, she hurriedly summoned all the family members.

As soon as they came in, they found Elena perfectly conscious and able to speak of St. Rita's vision, of her sudden cure and of other words she had heard during that vision. Having asked for something to eat, they brought her a large cup of coffee and scrambled eggs, which she consumed without any trouble. Meanwhile her relatives sent for Monsignor Mauro, the Dean, right away and Elena after telling him everything, asked permission to have a new statue of St. Rita placed on the spot indicated by the Saint. The Dean agreed forthwith and Elena's father ordered the statue from the Guacci firm at Lecce. A few days afterwards Monsignor Mauro received another proof of the absolute reality of those visions and of Elena's honesty and accuracy in reporting them.

We quote from her note-book: "On Friday night, November 8, 1921, Jesus appeared to her in a white garment and from His wounded Heart, which was quite visible, a beam of light encircled her head leaving thereon a trace of burnt hair. Jesus gave her to understand that those rays represented His loving invitation to suffer in atonement for the sins of the world. Elena was so frightened on account of the sparks encircling her head, that, jumping from the bed, she ran to the adjoining room, where her sisters were sleeping, but she fainted on reaching the threshold. Her sister Emma, who had heard the noise, got up, and, on crossing the door in search of matches to strike a light, she stumbled over Elena's body. Her sisters picked her up, made her lie down on their bed and, in the morning, they sent for the Dean. Monsignor Mauro told us that, after making a close inspection, he actually saw there was a strip of burnt hair on Elena's head. He picked up some of that hair which he still keeps."

Elena's hair was both long and thick. On the afternoon of November 9, Elena was to go to confession at the Institute of the Sisters of the Most Precious Blood. Her sister Emma, as usual, combed her hair and parted it into two long braids. By that time the Sisters had already heard of the phenomenon of the burnt hair from Monsignor Mauro. So as soon as Elena came in, the Superior, Sister Rosa Migali, made her sit down and told her they wished to take a look at her hair. Elena hesitated a while, but, since the Superior was insistent, and since she herself was unable to lift her arm, she let the Superior remove her veil and examine the hair. According to the note-book, Elena, at that moment prayed for some sign that would convince the Sisters of the truth of what had taken place.

Suddenly she felt as if an invisible hand had torn from her head the right braid which in fact had fallen at the very feet of Mother Superior. Quite amazed and terrified, she picked it up and placed it on Elena's knees, saying: "See, this is one of your braids: How about it? Did you cut it?" Local physicians examined the braid and reported that it was torn from the very root and that a hand mark was visible where the braid knot was thicker. On the following day all the missing hair was again in its place and was rearranged like the normal braid.

Faith is an essential condition for getting miracles because it glorifies God. A lively faith no matter how small, will always obtain them. We do find in Elena Aiello that a living, boundless, childlike faith in Jesus was habitual with her. No wonder then —as we shall see—that the supernatural became normal with her.

All that we have related so far excited very quickly the keen interest of Elena's fellow citizens. Her plea for St. Rita's devotions to be held in Montalto and for a statue to be placed in the Church of San Domenico, had met with the approval of her Confessor, Monsignor Mauro, who was also Dean of the Montalto Collegiate Chapter. However, don Angelo Bonelli, Pastor of Mount Carmel Church, and the Chapter's Treasurer, objected because he had thought for some time to establish that devotion in his own parish. The only reason why he hadn't done so, was because he didn't have enough money to pay for the statue.

Anyone who was acquainted with Sister Elena must have been impressed by the frank way of speaking her mind. When conversing she would fix her bright eyes on you with a glance that seemed to go through you. "Let your speech be yes, yes: no, no: and that which is over and above these, is of evil." (Matt. V,37). No quibbling or duplicity ever entered her mind: the deceitful way of saying "yes" and "no" at the same time was repugnant to her.

To honesty of mind she joined purity of intention and a courage that made her extraordinarily strong in her activities. By this time she no longer entertained any doubt concerning the truth of her visions because both her Confessor and the members of her family had checked and guaranteed the various events. She was waiting for St. Rita to completely cure her of her sore shoulder just as she had already done for the cancer of the stomach. Meanwhile she firmly stated to don Bonelli that she would loyally carry out St. Rita's request and that she would do so even at the cost of appealing to the Archbishop, if necessary. Realizing that it was useless to insist any further, don Bonelli forthwith placed an order for a Statue of St. Rita with the Malocore firm in Lecce.

Elena's reaction was considered impudent, disrespectful, and disobedient to clergy directives. The poor patient heard what was going on: she felt very bad indeed, but reacted now and then with that lively spirit so characteristic of her. That painful situation lasted a long time until the Archbishop of Cosenza, on being informed by the clergy, instructed the Dean, Monsignor Mauro, to be firm because only one Church was to hold St. Rita's devotions in the same town. To young Elena he wrote: "Miss Aiello, do pray to God not to be a victim to diabolical illusions!"

There is no need to stress the gravity of that situation in view of the implied threat of censure and of consequent loss of reputation. However, in response to another letter from Elena, the Archbishop did permit the Aiello family to keep their Statue in their home. Other arrangements would have to be made for the Church of Mt. Carmel. When St. Rita's Statue arrived, it was placed in Elena's house in a niche purposely made by her brother-in-law, Giovanni Ferrari. The Shepherd of the Cosenza Archidiocese at the time was the Most Reverend Thomas Trussoni (1912-1934). According to Father F. Russo, the whole course of his administration was a thorny one, from the very beginning, due to the evil times of prevailing sectarianism and to the deaths caused by the First World War. Like a good Shepherd, he restrained the hatreds by the humility and charity of his great heart and he was a consoling angel to people in affiiction and desolation on account of relatives lost during the war.

A man of God, in the full sense of the word, he could draw and charm souls by the very goodness of his heart and by his kind ways. A former professor of Moral Theology in the Como Seminary, and related to that Apostle of Charity, the Servant of God, don Luigi Guanella of Como, he possessed all the qualities for the discernment and direction of the most privileged souls, as well as the energy for upholding the kingdom of God by means of his evangelical prudence. Later on, he was to choose his own Vicar General, Monsignor Angelo Cironi as Elena's Spiritual Director and Moderator of the Institute. Within a few years he was to welcome and protect Sister Elena's activities by giving her—as we shall see—wise regulations against the danger of useless and harmful publicity concerning the extraordinary events we are going to relate. It is easy to see how prudently Archbishop Trussoni acted with regard to Elena if we compare his first severe command, coupled with apparent indifference, to his thoughtful consideration and esteem he ever entertained for her life and labors later on.

The Congregation of the Sister Minims of the Passion of Our Lord Jesus Christ found in Archbishop Thomas Trussoni the enlightened Shepherd who permitted, protected, helped and blessed their foundation and the first steps that are ever so hard to take. One day when Elena, though suffering, called on the Archbishop, His Excellency, bidding her good-bye, assured her of his prayers either for a healty recovery or for her complete resignation to God's Holy Will. He also exhorted her to accept all disappointments and sorrows as so many drops from Our Lord's bitter chalice.

St. Rita's Statue stayed in Elena's house up to the time she lived in Montalto, but, when she moved to Cosenza in 1927, to begin her mission, it was transferred to the Church of San Domenico to the very niche that Elena had indicated where it is presently standing. In the meantime, Elena, after her first recovery through St. Rita's intercession, took off the probation habit of the Sisters of the Most Precious Blood and put on, in fulfillment of her vow, the habit worn by St. Rita's nuns at Cascia. She kept wearing it until the time she selected the new one for the Congregation she had established.

Both her bodily sufferings and the more severe ones of the soul served to refine her spirit and to prepare her for the mission to which God had called her. In the course of the year 1922, Our Lord frequently admonished her to accept a new way of suffering. Elena spoke of it to her Confessor. "You are going to suffer, but fear not. Yours shall not be a malady but only the symbol of charity. I shall permit you to experience My very sadness and on Friday you will be more united to Me." During that winter four Passionist Fathers conducted a Mission directed by Father Ildefonso who was very well-known and esteemed throughout the Cosenza Archdiocese. A Religious of culture and great faith, he charmed and stirred the congregation by his exemplary life and by the force of his eloquence. The Passion of Our Lord, being the theme of his discourses, appealed very much to Elena's devout nature. At the end of the Mission, Elena disclosed her mind to him. Probably Elena's notes, which had been previously seen by Emma, her sister, but seemingly lost, found their way into Father Ildefonso's hands. In those notes Elena had written down whatever Our Lord and St. Rita had communicated to her. She received both light and encouragement from Very Rev. Father Ildefonso.

Now, just at the time when different opinions were being circulated concerning Elena, on account of the Statue's annoying story and of St. Rita's repeated apparitions, which she had duly confided to her Confessor, this is what happened. On the second day of March 1923, the first Friday of the month, an extraordinary event took place which was to make Elena known to very many people even those far away. That phenomenon was to recur every year even up to the time of her death.

On the morning of the second day of March, after Holy Communion, she heard an inner voice foretelling her of the new kind of suffering that Our Lord had chosen for her. May I now report from notes in the second copy book that I have with me. "On the first Friday in March, about 3 o'clock in the afternoon, while lying in bed on account of the painful cancerous wound on her left shoulder, and while reading the ninth Friday in honor of St. Francis of Paola, Our Lord appeared to her in a white garment and wearing a crown of thorns. On being asked if she was willing to suffer with Him, and on being assured of her consent, Our Lord removed the crown from His Head and placed it on Elena's head. Then and there a large quantity of blood started to flow. Our Lord told her He wished her to suffer for the conversion of sinners and for the many sins of impurity. He wanted her to be a victim in order to appease Divine Justice.

A certain woman, by the name of Rosaria, a family servant, was about to leave the house when she heard loud wailing in Elena's room. Wishing to know what was going on, she entered the room and seeing a lot of blood she feared that Elena had been killed. So she ran at once to warn the family. All of them with Emma, their sister, hurried to the room. On seeing so much blood they sent for Dr. Turano, for all the local physicians, for Dean Mauro and for several other priests.

Dr. Adolfo Turano started performing some lavages, but the blood kept oozing out of the head. At last, after three hours of intermittent bleeding, the phenomenon suddenly stopped. They were simply astonished, confused and badly shaken, because they were at a loss to explain what had happened. On the second Friday in March, before 3 o'clock in the afternoon, Dr. Adolfo Turano came back with several other people in order to check whether that phenomenon would recur. As a matter of fact the same bleeding took place at exactly the same hour. The Doctor tried to absorb the blood with some cloth, but, on touching the sore spot, the irritation of the skin caused all the pores to open and produced intense pain. Some little pieces of the skin would even stick to the cloth. For over three hours the blood kept flowing intermittently.

Thinking that perhaps the phenomenon was caused by religious obsession, her Confessor removed the Crucifix from the room on the third Friday in March, and forbade her to read any book dealing with the Passion of Jesus. In spite of that precaution the bleeding phenomenon took place at the same time and in the same way.

Mrs. D. Virginia Manes, a lady from the town of San Benedetto Ulano and mother of Dr. Aristodemo Milano, was sent by her son to verify that fact and to absorb some of the blood with a handkerchief. Accordingly, the moment she remained alone with Elena, she wiped her brow with a cloth. Then she folded and preserved it suspecting all along that her illness might be contagious. After returning to San Benedetto she discovered that the handkerchief was thoroughly clean with no trace of any blood. On hearing this report from his mother, Dr. Milano became a convert and was baptized.

In response to Elena's complaints about all she was going through on account of her bleeding, Our Lord in a vision assured her that it was He Who wished her to suffer, because she was to be a victim for the sins of the world. She shouldn't resent the fact that the Crucifix had been taken away from her, because He was ever present in her heart. As a proof of this He would give her a visible sign by making the wounds of His Passion to appear in her body. In fact on the last Friday in March, Jesus said to Elena, whose body was a mass of wounds: "You too must be like Me, because you are to be the victim for many a sinner, and you must appease My Father's Justice for their salvation.

About five o'clock Jesus greeted her: "My child, behold how much I suffer. I have shed all my blood for the world and yet everything goes to ruin. Nobody pays any attention to its countless crimes. See how bitterly I suffer for the wrongs and contempt I receive from so many wicked and immoral people." Elena replied: "And what can I do, my Jesus? Unless You come in person, no one will believe me." Jesus replied: "There are so many sinners whose obstinacy is the determinant cause for My Justice. But, my child, don't feel discouraged, because you will see Me again about one o'clock, and tell your Confessor I will give him a sign on Friday at 2 o'clock." Having said this, He disappeared.

On the following Friday, besides all the other wounds on her hands and feet, the wound on her side also came into sight. On Good Friday the phenomenon started exactly at noon. About six o'clock the procession of the Passion Mysteries was passing under the balcony of Elena's house. The sign that had been promised to the Confessor consisted in this—that Elena was to get up from bed at once perfectly conscious and able to watch the procession from the balcony. When the Statue of the Corpus of Jesus was being carried under the balcony, Elena became unconscious once more, while tears of blood were dripping from her eyes.

Some of the tears dripped on the head of her sister Ida who was standing on the lower balcony. At that moment Ida turning to Jesus complained that He had reserved such a heavy cross for her family on account of the large crowds that were calling and ever upsetting their home. The following night Our Lord warned Ida in her sleep, not to complain further about that cross, because Elena was bound to suffer for the salvation of many sinners. Only then Ida understood she should not complain since that was Elena's Mission. The Confessor, who had carefully marked down every thing, became convinced, after so much evidence, that the phenomenon was not caused by auto suggestion.

As soon as the phenomenon was over, Elena regained consciousness, but, after the procession moved on, the wounds on her feet, on the knees, on her side and on her right arm became wide open and very painful up to the month of June. On the Feast Day of Corpus Christi the wounds became still more painful and bleeding more profusely. Then, after a while, the wounds completely healed.

We have already emphasized that real holiness consists in doing God's Holy Will, in practicing charity and love by the complete dedication of self to God and to our neghbor. All the above mentioned events did in no way interfere with Elena's extraordinary activity, nor with the fulfillment of her duties as Foundress and Superior General of a new Religious Community. No curiosity seeker was ever permitted to be present while she was undergoing the Good Friday agony. The doors to her house were firmly locked, and on Holy Saturday morning, Sister Elena was already at her usual post of prayer, work and responsibility, apparently as if nothing unusual had happened to her.

Such uncommon events did not make it any easier for her in her relations with Church Authorities. Indeed, at times, they were a source of bitter experience and humiliations. Just the same people kept calling on her whenever they were in trouble and before making any important decisions. Sometimes it happened that people, anxious to visit her, would ask those in the know for the address of Sister Elena or Sister Elena Aiello. Imagine their surprise when they were told that such a person was unknown to them. However, it was sufficient to mention some of the well-known events like "The Sister who sweats blood" to be immediately told: "Oh, you are looking for the holy Nun" and to get the precise information. That was how Sister Elena was popularly known.

CHAPTER FOUR

Her Purulent Shoulder Is Instantly Healed

ON SEVERAL OCCASIONS Elena foretold she was going to be cured of the painful wound on her shoulder, and so we read in one of her letters to Monsignor Mauro, dated May 10, 1924.

"Reverend Father:

"Yesterday, about three o'clock in the afternoon, Jesus appeared to me saying: 'My beloved daughter, do you wish to get well or to go on suffering?' 'My Jesus,' I replied, 'one feels so good when suffering with You. However, do whatever You wish.' 'Well,' Jesus went on, 'You shall recover, but I want you to know that every Friday I shall permit you to be in a state of depression, so that you may stay closer to Me.' So saying, He disappeared.

Begging a memembrance in your holy prayers, and humbly kissing your hand, I am

Your most humble servant in Jesus Christ,
ELENA AIELLO"

A day or so before May 22, Dr. Adolfo Turano was sent for by the family because the patient's condition had become worse. Elena told him again the story of her vision of St. Rita who had promised to heal her on the afternoon of May 22. Considering how sick she was, the Doctor concluded that what Elena was telling him was simply the effect of hallucination, and so he cautioned the family.

On May 22 at 2:45 P.M., Elena, after being dressed by her

sister Emma, was carried down, with considerable effort, to the parlor on the lower floor and laid down on a sofa opposite St. Rita's Statue. Now this is what happened according to Emma's deposition made to Counsellor Di Napoli on October 30, 1961. Showing unusual courage, Elena was pulling out some of the worms out of her sore shoulder with the help of a mirror and of some splinters. What Mrs. Alina Caracciolo, a resident of Verona Palazzolo has told you is true. We were able to learn the secret of the worms from Giovannina who had been spying on Elena's movements. When for compassion sake I volunteered to extract them, I imitated Elena by using splinters. I would first cut the skin all around the deep seated wound and then, by using the splinters, I would force the worms out. But the more I pulled out, the more remained inside. Afterwards, according to instructions, I would lay some yellow powder thereon, but to no avail. Elena looked quite resigned while enduring that torture, but her faith in St. Rita was amazing. She felt perfectly sure she would be cured, but few people could believe it. After all she had been suffering for three long years.

In a dream Elena had on the night of May 21, 1924, St. Rita told her she would make her well on the following day at three o'clock in the afternoon. During the month of May, we were reciting the Rosary, as usual, and some of the neighbors were there including Carlo Taormina, a notary public and a frequent guest, who thought a great deal of Elena.

During that year Elena had been very much weakened by the serious crisis she had endured during the month of April. In order to carry her down to the lower floor we had to take her in our arms, like a paralyzed person, and then we would seat her on that sofa . . . opposite St. Rita's Statue.

We waited . . . we were trembling, restless, excited, unable to say a word. After reciting the Rosary in front of the Statue—the niche door being open—Elena began praying in a tone of voice that was hardly audible: 'From your sanctuary of mercy, o Saint of the impossible, and patron of desperate cases, do turn your eyes of mercy on me, and behold the anguish overwhelming me, the misfortune and misery gripping me: for there is no other one I may turn to. Withered is the source of my tears;

even prayer is dying on my poor lips. Hope is all that is left to me. O Saint Rita, powerful and glorious, come to my aid, and, in this direst need, grant me the grace I beg of you! You have promised it to me: You must grant it to me. You must not permit that I be called a liar!"

Then, by helping her, she got up and came close to the Statue. We felt the impression that the hand of St. Rita facing the Crucifix had turned towards Elena's hand, on the wounded side in order to lift it up, and that both the statue and the niche had been shaken by some sort of vibration. "I am cured, I am cured," cried out Elena to all of us who were perfectly astonished, but still skeptical. Then, without any help, she walked easily to the balcony. There, on seeing the widow of notary public Ceci, standing at a window on the opposite side, she lifted up her arms and exclaimed: "Donna Valentina, look, I am cured." When I asked her to show me her wound I found it sealed: a scar was all that could be seen.""

In the second note-book we read as follows: "During the night of May 21, 1924, I had a vision of St. Rita to whom I had so often prayed for the grace of recovery. I had duly complied with her request, but it didn't depend on me if the Statue was still in my house. She reassured me about her promise to cure me but she added that my suffering would continue. She then concluded: "Tomorrow after the Rosary, come close to my Statue and I will cure you." Being quite anxious but comforted, about three o'clock in the afternoon, after saying the Rosary with some of my sisters, with some friends and another relative, I left the sofa with the help of Emma and came close to the Statue. I was intently looking at her while praying. Suddenly I felt quite light and free to move. I stood up, feeling great joy in my heart, and on seeing others quite happy but puzzled, I said, "I am cured." Then I left them and went straight to the balcony. The moment I saw Donna Valentina Vescillo, I instinctively cried out to her as I lifted up my arms. "Just look! I am cured!" The wormy wound was no longer there."

CHAPTER FIVE

In Search of a Co-Worker

LET US NOW RESUME the trend of our notes. They lead us to Bucita, a tiny village amid chestnut trees, a section of the San Fili commune, and not so distant from Montalto. Here, within a large and exemplary Christian family, we find the young lady who is going to be Elena's faithful associate from the very beginning of her work, and who is destined later on to succeed her.

Gigia Mazza, born at Bucita on October 28, 1892, was the child of Santo, an honest workman and of Maria Guccione. Of their twelve children, four had enrolled as members of the glorious Order of the Minims. Fra Giovanni (born June 18, 1888), Father Beniamino (born November 20, 1893), an emigrant, served in the United States Army both in England and in France (1917-1918) then, upon returning to Italy, he entered the Order of San Francesco di Paola at Genoa and was ordained a Priest in Rome on July 3, 1927.

Father Francesco (born November 3, 1903) entered the Monastery adjoining Paola's Sanctuary when only twelve years of age. After serving in the Army, he finished his philosophy and theology course at Rome. After his ordination in 1930, he was Director of the Institute of the Minims (then on Pompei Square) until 1937. Back again at Paola, he was elected Provincial twice, 1945-1948 and 1955-1958.

Father Arturo (born December 1908) was ordained a Priest in 1932.

Elena's oldest sister Pasqualina, who died in 1918, was married to artisan Vincenzo Lagana. She saw two of her children follow their uncles into the same Order: Fra Giovanni (born 1911) and Father Biagio (born 1915). Her daughter Concetta entered Sister Elena's Congregation in 1930 and died in 1932. Behold a family especially devoted to San Francesco of Paola.

Pursuant to her desire to consecrate herself to God, Gigia was already thirty years old when she obtained her parents' consent in 1922, to enter the Congregation of the Sisters Reparatrix of the Sacred Heart in Naples. Earlier she had been prevented from leaving home, first by the World War and then by the death (1918) of her sister Pasqualina, who had left seven small children after her.

But her stay in Naples lasted only a few months (January 1-May 4, 1923) because of poor health from the very beginning. Then, following a relapse, the doctor ordered her to return home and take care of her health. It was precisely during Lent of that year that the extraordinary events, which we have previously related, were taking place. Perhaps at Bucita, that was nearby, more than in any other town of the province, people were talking about that Nun in Montalto who was so impressively partaking of Our Lord's Passion. Furthermore, Gigia, who had been entrusted by her family to Dr. Turano's care—a physician of the Aiello family and of Elena also—in her regular visits to Montalto, had a fine opportunity to get the right information. Thus, on the Friday after Eastern, she went with her mother to Elena's house to make her acquaintance and to seek some advice concerning her vocation. She wanted to know whether she should return to the Convent, which she had unwillingly left, and, whether God had other designs for her. She desired to be present during the time she was suffering of which she had heard so much, and which she believed to happen every Friday. With her usual simplicity, Elena replied that the suffering period had come to an end on Good Friday. She would have had to wait until the following year because a phenomenon of that kind would occur only during the Lenten Fridays in March.

Then she consoled her for having left the Convent, for she also had been compelled to leave her Congregation on account of her health, and had had to return home under the pressure of so much suffering. Elena didn't have to say much more on that point, because that sore on shoulder almost disfigured her. However—for Gigia's consolation—Elena said that, since God had permitted that much to happen, He must have done it, without doubt, for some motive which He would not fail to disclose later on. Comforted by these words, Gigia returned home with a lively hope for her future vocation. That was the beginning of the relations that were to bind ever more the young lady of Bucita to Elena. Everytime Gigia returned to Montalto to visit Dr. Tulano, she would call on Elena with whom, by this time, she talked quite confidentially. During Lent of 1924 she was present at the phenomenon that we have already described. During the month of May of that year, with the shoulder wound still tormenting her, Elena told Gigia to give up the idea of going back to her former Congregation in Naples. For she would become a Nun indeed, but only for the purpose of starting a new kind of work with her. Instinctively Gigia couldn't help thinking: "She is dying and she expects to establish a Religious Community!" To which Elena quickly retorted: "Don't worry because St. Rita will cure me on the 22nd of this month." She further told her that she intended to rest for a week or so in her house at Bucita.

Gigia related everything to her family. One of her neighbors, Mrs. Angelina Asta Ferrari, quite ill on account of two tumors, on hearing the story about Elena, begged Gigia to interest Elena in her case, so that she might be cured through her prayers. Wishing to please her, Gigia returned to Montalto in company with Michele Ferrari—the sick woman's husband—and his mother. Elena agreed to their request and gave them a picture of St. Rita and some rose leaves from Cascia to be applied on the sore spot. On returning home, Michele Asta and his mother couldn't help saying to Gigia: "We have come all this way and we have wasted our time."

For they were depressed at seeing Elena's pitiful condition. "How could anyone who is so sick be able to cure other people? Anyway, as they returned home, trusting in St. Rita, they applied both her picture and the rose leaves on Angelina's sore spot. During the night both tumors burst open. In the morning when

Professor Santoro came in for the operation, he found that the patient was fast recovering.

When Gigia heard of Elena's extraordinary recovery, on May 22, she returned to Montalto and found her in perfect health. Elena promised she would shortly be with her at Bucita. Actually an acute stage of periostitis had developed, as a result of a sore mouth, for a long time, which was caused by the steady use of ice during the three years she had been bedridden. In the following month of November, she decided to go to Dr. Chimenti, the dentist at Cosenza, because she couldn't stand the severe pain any longer. On her way, the bus broke down near Bucita, so Elena availed herself of the opportunity to call on Gigia.

That was the very first time Elena made a visit to the house of Sister Gigia in Bucita. As soon as repairs were made, the bus reached Cosenza, where the dentist found it necessary to extract all of Elena's molars. Thus the dreadful pain, which she had endured for such a long time, came to an end. Also another small periostitis operation was performed on a molar which had been cut in two by a poorly qualified physician at Montalto, on the previous year.

After a month or so, on returning to Cosenza, for another medical appointment, she had another opportunity to stop at Bucita. There, when leaving Sister Gigia, Elena told the mother, zia Maria, that God wished her to begin a special work jointly with her daughter Sister Gigia and that, for this reason, the parents should give their consent for her departure to Cosenza. Her mother replied that, in that case, her family would readily consent, but that, they were unwilling to do so in case she wanted to return to another Religious Community, since the former test had not proved successful.

CHAPTER SIX

The Little Flower Walks at Her Side

WE HAVE CULLED the following items from the second note-book in our possession. "In 1926 the sufferings on the Fridays in March and on Good Friday recurred regularly. During the visions Our Lord had manifested His desire to have the work started. In the meantime a house had been offered to Elena by Michael Stillo of Cosenza for some kind of a charitable work. However, Dean Mauro had urged Elena to establish a Home for the Aged at Montalto. At first Elena had agreed to, but she declined to do so later on, when she found out that the Dean intended her to start that foundation together with the Sisters of the Most Precious Blood of the Marigliano Institute. To her, that didn't seem to be God's Holy Will. Sister Gigia also, on hearing from Elena about the new situation, refused to go to Montalto under those circumstances.

For the sake of a tranquil conscience, Elena wrote to Monsignor Sironi, her extraordinary Spiritual Director, for the benefit of his advice. Monsignor replied by urging her to go to Cosenza and acquaint the Archbishop with the contents of her letter to him. At this time since Elena had to go to Cascia with her sister Giovannina for the fulfillment of a vow she had made to St. Rita, the Mother Superior there, Sister Teresa, insistently requested her to come and she was anxiously waiting for her. But Elena decided first to go to Cosenza in order to consult the Archbishop and then later on to go to Rome.

She gave a full account of everything to the Most Reverend Trussoni, Archbishop of Cosenza. His Excellency understood full well Elena's mind and advised her to follow God's Will independently of any other person. Then for the sake of a tranquil conscience, he suggested that, on arriving to Rome, she should call on the Jesuit Father Marchetti, give him his letter of introduction and follow his enlightened counsel. In Rome Father Marchetti fully concurred with the Archbishop's mind, and, for his part too, he insisted that she should start the Work to which God was calling her and not to pay attention to anybody else.

So in company with her fine hostess Countess Sacconi, she went to Cascia to fulfil her vow before St. Rita's Urn. The Abbess of that Convent tried to persuade Elena to stay there as one of the Sisters and, as an inducement, lodged her in a tiny cell inside the cloister. But Elena felt no attraction to that rigid cloistered life, and consequently she urged both her sister and the Countess, who were in the guest house, to make ready for an early departure for Rome. From Rome she went to Cosenza, and there she told the Archbishop she desired to go away from her native town on account of the publicity that was going on during the time of her sufferings. The Archbishop readily agreed with Elena and exhorted her to carry out her plan. Taking advantage of her stay in Cosenza, she called on Michele Stillo in order to make arrangements about that house he had so often offered to her. But nothing came out of it.

Returning to Cosenza Elena realized that to make a start in Cosenza it was imperative for her to rent a house for the time being. At Montalto, don Duilio Ceci had also been thinking of opening a home for the War Orphans with Elena's cooperation, but this time also, Elena refused as she had previously done with the Dean. In 1927, during the course of her sufferings Our Lord again made clear to Elena that she was to start at once the work He wanted jointly with Sister Giggia.

After her period of suffering was over, Elena requested Sister Gigia to proceed with her to Cosenza. However, Gigia reminded her that her brother, Beniamino, was about to be ordained a Priest, and that therefore it was advisable to talk about that matter later on, i.e., after the First Mass had been celebrated at Bucita during that Summer. Profiting by this circumstance Elena communicated to Sister Gigia her desire to spend a month in her company at Bucita, because the Doctors had ordered a change of climate and had actually prescribed that she should breathe the mild air of that lovely village.

Elena went to Bucita during the month of August of that very year, 1927, and helped Gigia make preparations for the First Mass of Father Beniamino who was due to arrive towards the beginning of September.

That celebration was attended not only by all of the Mazza brothers, but also by the Very Reverend Father Pietro Lalli, Corrector General of the Order, the Very Reverend Father Bartolomeo Verde, Provincial Corrector and by many other Priests and Religious of the Basilica of Paola, who welcomed the opportunity to get acquainted with Elena. On the very day of that Feast, all the Religious made an excursion to Montalto in order to visit Elena's house and have a look at the famous braid.

During the month of September, Sister Gigia's brothers stayed home and it was then they decided it was time for Elena to go to Cosenza and start the work she had so often mentioned. While discussing the type of charitable work that should be initiated, they concluded that the best thing to do was to let Divine Providence clearly show the way and to consider the first donation as a sure sign thereof. On that same month of September, Sister Gigia's brothers called on the Archbishop to secure his permission for Elena's and Gigia's domicile in Cosenza. The Archbishop did not fail to state to them the difficulties inherent to such work, especially on account of the extraordinary events that were causing such a sensation. However, he was assured that as far as the work was concerned, only the plan manifested by Divine Providence would be followed and that they would keep all the extraordinary events hidden from popular curiosity.

With that assurance, the Archbishop gave permission to the two Sisters to establish their domicile in Cosenza. They also talked with the Vicar, Monsignor Sironi, who pledged his help and spiritual direction to the Sisters with whom he was already acquainted.

The Sisters arrived in Cosenza in November and took lodging in a house owned by Canon Colistro, who was conducting a boarding school for students. For that reason, he was very much interested in providing lodging to Sisters who could assume management of the school. In the meantime through the Fusaro family, quite friendly to the two Sisters, they heard that the Cavalcanti house, close to the Normal School, might be rented. But after settling the rental price, Mr. Cavalcanti refused to sign the contract on the plea that he needed a guarantee from the Sister's parents.

The following day Sister Gigia returned home, whereas Sister Elena, who was a guest of the Fusaro family, stayed until the following day. The morning after, she walked to the nearby Church of St. Nicholas, and she prayed for a long time there in front of the Statue of St. Teresina of the Infant Jesus. Then about 2 o'clock that afternoon, on her way to the bus that was to take her back to Montalto, she met with one of her relatives, Engineer Giacinto della Cananea who firmly dissuaded her from renting the Cavalcanti house because it was unfit for her purpose.

Entering the bus, Sister Elena took a seat close to the door and kept thinking how to solve that problem of the house. Her mind turned to her Patron Saints and particularly to St. Teresa of the Infant Jesus. She was beseeching them to come to her aid in that pressing need. While absorbed in prayer she heard the bus door open, and, turning around, she saw a Carmelite Nun, who asked her if she was looking for a house. Thinking she was one of the Sisters from Castrovillari, Sister Elena kissed her hand and told her how hard it was to find a suitable building for what she had in mind. The Nun, sweetly smiling, invited her to get out of the bus, saying: "Come, I will show you the house."

Thereupon Sister Elena alighted from the bus and asked Engineer della Cananea to notify her family that she would return the following day because she had to go with a Nun who wanted to give her some information about a house. Along the way the mysterious Nun indicated the exact location of a house on the second Revocati lane, and she specified also the landlady's name, i.e., Marie De Rosa. Then she added that the lease on the house had already been pledged to a postal official for 260 lire a month. But, concluded the Nun, if you go in, you will see that she will prefer you for only 250 lire a month.

When they reached the corner of the second lane, the Nun pointed to the balcony of that house to Sister Elena, and then she became suddenly transfigured with a Crucifix in her hands and with a gorgeous bouquet of roses streaming from the Crucifix. The vision became evanescent, then gradually shrinking, it disappeared altogether as if in a haze. Overcoming her natural excitement, Elena, on reaching Mrs. De Rosa's residence, inquired about the house and was told by that nice lady that she was very happy indeed to rent it with a 10 lire reduction. Through the good offices of Pietro Fasano, who also advanced the 250 lire in Elena's name, the contract was signed that same evening. The following morning Elena called on the Archbishop informing him of all that had happened the previous day. The Archbishop exhorted Sister Elena to dedicate her first house in Cosenza to that Saint of Lisieux.

CHAPTER SEVEN

Her Dream About Three Little Girls

RETURNING TO MONTALTO, Sister Elena informed Sister Gigia that the problem of the house was settled. They both agreed to go back to Cosenza towards the end of the year. So, they moved to Cosenza after the Christmas holy days and took possession of the house. They had received quite a number of invitations for the New Year's Eve celebration from families of their acquaintaince, but they preferred to stay at home. Having no provisions of any kind, they ate some cake on a piece of paper and went to bed.

After a day or so, they decided to return home in order to straighten out everything and to assemble whatever was necessary for the furnishing of the house. So, after placing all items on a wagon, very early in the morning of January 17, Sister Elena Aiello, solely intent upon following God's Will, quitetly left her native town and proceed to Cosenza. She acted thus because she knew that plans had been made to prevent her from leaving Montalto.

On entering the city, her first visit was to the Statue of the Little Flower in St. Nicholas' Church. There she heard Holy Mass and received Communion. When going out of the Church, she met Dean Mauro, who had purposely come from Montalto to persuade Elena to return home. But Elena was firm in her resolution. "If I get along well enough, I shall continue; if not, I shall come home."

On January 29, the Feast Day of St. Francis de Sales, they began the apostolate to which God had called them. Their first effort was to give instructions to children of the common people, the more so because that work had been rather neglected in that district. They assembled about one hundred of them, gave them religious instructions, cared for them in the nursery, taught them how to sew and embroïder and prepared them for their First Holy Communion.

Burning with a desire to estend their important work everywhere, they even visited the difficult Panebianco district where the Protestants were conducting their propaganda. The two Nuns went from house to house in search of little boys and girls in order to gather them in the Church of Our Lady of Loreto, teach them the Catechism and prepare them for First Holy Communion. Many a time Sister Elena even went inside the protestant hall, during the assembly hour, and, in the very presence of the Minister, she exhorted those poor people to go back to the Catholic Church.

Many a person, who was living in sin, had the marriage validated: others received Holy Communion late in life and a few children were baptised. There lived at the time a young fellow, who was the terror of the whole district, on account of his nightly plundering through the nearby farms. They nicknamed him "Ciccio the thief." He was about fourteen years old, at the time the two Nuns got hold of him, and they coaxed him to come to Church for Cathechism instructions. True to his word he went promptly to Church for fifteen days, during which time he was well instructed for First Holy Communion. On the very day of his First Communion he also received the Sacrament of Confirmation with such faith and religious fervor as to astonish all those who had known him. And it was during that time of spiritual fervor that God called him by broncho-pneumonia to his eternal reward in heaven. That was exactly eight days after his First Communion.

During the first months of 1928 the Nuns developed their work so quickly that they were compelled to look right away for another house better suited to their new needs. Sister Elena's sufferings recurred regularly in March 1928 just as in the previous years, but Sister Gigia locked her up in the attic in order to hide her away from the attention of the authorities as well as of the many people who knew her.

When such persons inquired for news, Sister Gigia invariably answered that Elena had moved away to a solitary place far away from Cosenza. As soon as the Fusaro family heard from Elena's father that he had gone to Cosenza to visit his sick daughter, they quickly proceeded to the Revocati street to witness the phenomenon. However, Sister Gigia, keeping her promise to the Church authorities, permitted no one to go inside the house. Even the police force, after much pleading with the Archbishop, got nowhere.

During the summer months a Mrs. Abate, while making arrangements with Sister Elena for one of her daughters' trousseau, suggested to both Nuns that it might be advantageous if they moved to the Caselli House in Vecchia Street. For it was quite spacious and better suited to their work. Counsellor Nicholas—the Caselli family lawyer—prepared the lease for a 450 lire monthly rental which they signed.

In the month of September, Sister Gigia's brothers who happened to be home, wired the entire Caselli House with an electrical system. After preparing a very frugal lunch, Sister Elena and Sister Gigia had to place the scant food on an old and wobbling table which was the only piece of furniture in the house. That was poverty indeed! An embroidery school was opened in those spacious quarters and quite a number of young ladies belonging to some of the best Cosenza families attended that course. In the meantime Elena was considering what specific work of charity she should start with. She talked it over with Sister Gigia and both decided to have Father Giovanni Corrao, O.F.M., offer up a Holy Mass on December 4 in honor of the Sacred Heart of Jesus in the nearby Church of St. Francis of Assisi. That very day, at noon, a Mr. Giovanni Zeni, who was sent by the Archbishop, came along with Rita Panno, an orphan child who lived in Portapiana. That gentleman was accompanied by Monsignor Sironi and, on surrendering the little girl, he pledged a monthly sum of fifty lire for her board. This he did in memory of his wife and he also gave a diamond pin which

Sister Elena sold for seven thousand lire and bought a small trousseau for little Rita.

A day or so afterwards Sister Elena had a night dream. She had just left the house to take to college two girls from Rossano who were temporarily boarding at the Caselli House. That school was close to the Grillo Library where a mail box is fastened to a steel fence. There she saw a man, dressed in black, holding three girls and looking for some Nun. The moment he saw Sister Elena, he begged her to take care of the three girls because, after their mother's death, they were suffering a great deal from an aunt who insisted on taking them down to the river almost every day. Sister Elena replied she felt quite worried about them but the man insisted she should have confidence in Divine Providence.

On awakening, Sister Elena related her dream to Sister Gigia. That very morning, when taking the girls to school, she met, on that very spot, the man with the three girls saying the same words she had heard in her dream. Very deeply affected, Sister Elena embraced the three little girls and took them home with her. Here are their names: Lilliana Rende, age 7, Ernestina, 4, and Sandrina, 3. During that same month Assunta Ruffolo, age 8, and Anna Miranda, 4, were also admitted.

On December 19, Archbishop Trussoni bid his Vicar to bless the chapel and to take along with him a retarded girl by the name of Gina Martino, daughter of a war refugee (1915-1918). Monsignor Vicar expressed his satisfaction with the Nuns' activities, and blessed their work and holy desires in the name of the Archbishop. The house was dedicated to St. Teresa of the Infant Jesus. Blessed by God and encouraged by Church Authorities, that work earned the enthusiastic approval of the entire City of Cosenza which fostered and supported it with admirable christian charity. Barely one year afterwards, twenty-four girls were sheltered there.

We should not forget to mention the admirable interest of the Mazza brothers in that Institution. Outstanding also is the strong faith that animated the entire life of Sister Elena. St. Paul's sentence was rooted in her soul and it was firmly believed by her: "To them that love God, all things work together unto good." (Rom. VIII, 28)

She had full faith in Divine Providence. "Fear not little flock, for it has pleased your Father to give you a Kingdom. Sell what you possess and give alms. Make to yourselves bags which grow not old, a treasure in heaven which fails not, where no thief approaches, nor moth corrupts, for where your treasure is, there is your heart also." (Luke, XII, 32). Similar words we read in the Sermon on the Mount. "Be not solicitous for your life, what you shall eat, or what you shall drink . . . behold the birds of the air . . . behold the lilies of the field . . . how much more will he clothe you, O you of little faith . . . your heavenly Father knows you need all these things. Seek you, therefore, first the Kingdom of God and His justice and all these things shall be added to you. Be not solicitous therefore for tomorrow, for the morrow will be solicitous for itself. Sufficient for the day is the evil thereof." (Matthew VI, 25-34)

So trusting in Divine Providence, Elena started from scratch the work God wanted her todo, and from day to day, with great calm, she sought to fulfil her duties, both as a Religious and as a Superior, to the little ones and to her Community. She had serenely awaited and, at last, she had received from heaven the inspiration concerning the nature of her work and how to set it in motion.

Where a person, without faith, sees merely the chance, a soul, that is imbued with God's presence, and diligently prays to know His Will in order to humbly and gratefully fulfil it, that soul does perceive the real action of Divine Providence. Elena's whole life was a constant proof of that burning faith, of that unalterable calm of the spirit, which comes from a complete surrender to the Almighty Who is so fatherly and merciful to us. Hers was an active faith made ever stronger by the practice of charity in Christ.

A great Russian writer competently describes that truth in these words. "Endeavor to feel an active and continual love for your neighbor. As you make progress in this way of love, you shall be evermore convinced of God's existence and of the immortality of your soul. And if you reach complete self-denial for your neighbor's sake, then, without doubt, you shall have acquired a perfect faith without even the shadow of a doubt. That is an ordinary experience, and it is a true one indeed."

That kind of supernatural charity was now being practiced towards the little abandoned girls for whom Divine Providence has a special preference. Sister Elena loved to recall that Gospel passage in which Jesus blessed the children: "Then were little children presented to Him, that He should impose hands upon them and pray. And the disciples rebuked them. But Jesus said to them: "Suffer the little children, and forbit them not to come to Me, for the Kingdom of heaven is for such. Then He laid His hands on them." (Matthew XIX, 13)

That supernatural charity makes us love those who need our help for Jesus' sake. That love induced Elena to be a mother to those little ones who, quite often, had never seen their parents, and to lead them to the supernatural life. In the morning the little ones had to be cleaned, washed, clothed and assisted during the entire day. Also provision had to be made to embrace with ardor such a mission—difficult indeed—unless one's heart is burning with supernatural love, unless one loves Jesus and all those He entrusts to us.

That supernatural charity causes us to fulfil with complete responsibility our assigned mission. It is also ever vigilant over self, preventing and rooting out, from the very beginning, any human aspiration or feeling, which might gradually turn a good charitable deed into a simple act of human sympathy or even worse. We should ever remember the words of Jesus to the Apostles, who had inquired of Him: "Who is the greatest in the Kingdom of heaven?" So He called a little child to Him and set the child in front of them. Then He said: "I tell you solemnly, unless you change and become like little children, you will never enter the Kingdom of Heaven. Anyone who welcomes a little child like this in My name welcomes Me. But anyone, who shall scandalize one of these little ones who have a faith in Me, would be better drowned in the depths of the sea with a great millstone around his neck." (Matt. XVIII, 1-6)

Concerning the above quotation from St. Matthew, St. John Chrysostom writes as follows in his 60th Homily: "No art is greater than that which is dedicated to the formation and training of a child's mind and character. Whoever is endowed with such ability should work harder than any painter or sculptor: for there is nothing more precious than a soul."

And the Russian writer, already quoted, makes the following observations that are quite to the point: "Take care that your behavior be always dignified every day, every hour, every moment. Lo, you just passed by a little boy: you were quite angry . . . a bad word escaped from your lips . . . there was some anger in your heart . . . you didn't notice that little boy, but he took notice of you: he watched you and your image so crude, so harsh, is perhaps now imprinted in his innocent heart. It is quite possible that you have unwillingly sown an evil seed in his heart. Perhaps that seed will grow up just because you made no restraint in presence of that little boy—just because you didn't try to foster a vigilant and active love within you. Love is a teacher, but you must learn how to get hold of it, because it is hard to get, and it is bought at a high price. For one must not love for a moment only, by chance: one must love for a lifetime."

Sister Elena was already prepared for this life of sacrifice and of supernatural love. Her shining faith of which she was gifted from her very childhood, her charity refined by suffering, and made secure and strong by the care of the sick and the dying as well as by her fervent prayers for the salvation of souls, made it possible, from the very beginning to give her work that supernatural directive which caused it to increase and yield that abundant fruit that everybody now sees and admires.

From the very beginning she carefully trained the young ladies who were to join her Community pretty soon in the work she had just started. This is why Elena selected, as a distinguishing mark, the charity of St. Francis of Paola, with the emblem of the Passion of Our Lord Jesus Christ, and named her Institute "Sister Minims of the Passion of Our Lord." Both that name and that emblem were already indicative of an actual program and they clearly pointed out the nature and purpose of the Institution to the young ladies who were called to the religious life.

CHAPTER EIGHT

A Scoundrel Runs for Cover

BY 1929 THE NUMBER of little orphans had climbed to 26. During the first months of the same year, the first two young aspirants arrived from Bucita: Carmelina Cribari, now superior of the House in San Fili and Emila Artura. An ex-Nun, Dolorosa da C., who had been specially recommended by a Priest, was shortly asked to leave. Right after Easter a lady doctor succeeded in demanding an investigation from Rome through the "Maternity and Infancy Institution."

"A woman, (Sister Elena) ill with T. B., was supposedly boarding old age people and little abandoned girls in her own house." The Prefecture appointed a Committee consisting of Dr. Mario Misasi, Francesco Misasi, and Dr. Volpe, Chief Accountant at the Prefecture. They ascertained the absolute falsehood of that accusation.

Sandrina Rende, the last of the three little sisters sheltered in December 1928, died on the First Friday of March 1930. Sister Elena was suddenly seized by the spell of one of those extraordinary phenomena while adorning with flowers the still body of that little angel. The Nuns picked her up and laid her on the bed where the phenomena took their usual course. About this time, the Prefect, Dr. Bianchetti and his wife, who were charitably disposed and sought to help the poor and the sick in every way, displayed special benevolence toward Sister Elena and her little girls. During her charitable activities, Lady Bianchetti desired and often enjoyed the company of Sister Elena who was thus reminded of bygone years in her native Montalto when she used to visit the poor and the sick and to offer them a word of consolation.

Occasionally St. Teresa of the Infant Jesus showed how pleased she was with the little Community, that bore her name, by giving a tangible proof of her protection and watchful presence. One day she appeared sweetly smiling to all the little ones who, while sewing in the work-room, were saying some prayers. Their noisy shouting brought Sister Elena hurriedly down from the upper floor while the little ones were loudly screaming: "We have seen the Carmelite Saint." On returning upstairs, Elena too saw St. Teresa who, from the threshold of her room, was smiling at her. In August 1930, though tortured by intense pain, she attended the celebration of the First Mass by Father Francesco Mazza at Bucita. Towards the end of September she was examined by Professor Falcone, and shortly after in Rome, by Professor Bastianelli who advised to have her appendix removed. It was only on November 16 that the operation was performed in the City Hospital of Cosenza, because Sister Elena had first wanted to finish the furnishing of the little house adjacent to the Church of St. Francis of Paola. That house was to be the residence of the Father Minims who at last had returned to Cosenza.

The third aspirant, Concetta Lagana, Sister Gigia's niece, came in December. On June 13, 1931, the group of the little ones increased by the arrival of an eleven month old girl. Her mother, who had been compelled to relinquish her, entrusted her to the Sisters' care, but she never came back. When, after diligent inquires, her name came to be known, that very same name Anna B.D., was given to that baby girl. Another girl was admitted on the following day.

A certain scoundrel by the name of Pasquale C., came down regularly from St. Vincenzo La Costa to Cosenza peddling cheese. He would take along his ragged little daughter and force her to go begging through the Panebianco district. Then, in the evening, he would tie her to a basket and take her back to the village. One day, in the neighborhood of the Caselli House, that villain was about selling his daughter for 30 lire to a young coachman. Elena, who had heard them bargaining, quickly notified Counsellor Arabia, across the street, and asked for his help. The two contemptible fellows suddenly vanished and left poor little Marietta C., alone, Sister Elena promptly took her home. The District Attorney, who had been notified of the whole case, authorized Sister to keep the little girl, in spite of any protest or demand from her father.

In August 1931, scarlet fever was raging in Cosenza. Ernestina Rende was stricken. Sister Elena brought all the girls to Bucita whereas the little invalid had to be quarantined. The cheese peddler came back from the nearby village and forcibly tried to abduct the little girl. But Sister Elena promptly and decisively frustrated his evil design by wresting her from his hands.

During a night dream Elena saw that the Cosenza house, where Sister Gigia and Sister Carmelina were staying, had been quarantined. Doctor V. Vercillo, on returning from Cosenza, told Sister Elena that he had actually seen the municipal guards on their way to disinfect the Sisters' dwelling at the Caselli House, but he couldn't say any more. Feeling uneasy, Elena proceeded to Cosenza at once. The house had been disinfected and locked. Anna B., had been quarantined and, since the two Nuns were in good health, Elena returned to Bucita the same day. During October, after the epidemic was completely over, all of the girls returned home and so the Community resumed its routine work at the Caselli House.

Cesare Guasti dedicated the translation of the "Imitation of Christ" to his daughter with these words, "In order that you may learn to love and to suffer in a christian manner, I recommend this book to you, O my Angelina, and you, when reading and meditating, remember your father." Then he appended the following verses: "Love—a worthy goal—you will find herein during serene fleeting hours: and solace to your heart in life's long suffering: Thus, as joy and sorrows come and go, forever lasting is the peace of him who trusts in God."

Truly, our short span of life is but one alternative of joys and sorrows. The story of any good work is a tale of frequent tribulations, incomprehensions and even persecutions from some quarters and of admiration, sympathy and support from the other side. But over and above all stands Divine Providence ever directing all things for the good of those who trust in God.

CHAPTER NINE

How Did the Money Get There?

CONSIDERING HER POVERTY, the house rental was a serious burden to Sister Elena. But here too, help came unexpectedly. The Rev. Prof. Carlo De Cardona, founder and director of the Rural Bank, offered to the Institute the old quarters of the Bank on Holy Spirit Street between the Church so named and the Street leading to the Prefecture. Sister Elena and Sister Gigia moved to the new house right away. Since the building was much larger, the number of the little orphans and of the Sisters increased. During August the Rev. Father Arturo Mazza offered up his First Mass at Bucita. Both Sister Elena and Sister Concetta Lagana hastened there to make the usual preparations, but, the latter became ill, and on being taken back to the Cosenza Hospital, breathed her last on August 15 at 10 o'clock. Sister Luisa Perna, who assisted Sister Elena to the very end and Sister Giulia Montemurro were admitted in November 1932.

Holy Year 1933—Sister Elena and Sister Gigia made their pilgrimage to Rome during that Autumn. The following Sisters were received in September 1934: Sister Angela Padula, Sister Modesta Petrone, Sister Teresa Infusino, Sister Filomena Santelli, Sister Maria Santelli and, on January 2, 1935, Sister Adelina Cristiano and Sister Laura Miceli.

The Most Reverend Roberto Nogara, the new Archbishop who had been appointed on August 27, 1934, made his entrance in Cosenza on January 6, 1935. His Excellency Archbishop Trussoni, who resigned, had left the Archdiocese a few months earlier, with the whole city turning out in a touching farewell demonstration. The new Shepherd was welcomed with great enthusiasm and affection. In his "History of the Archdiocese of Cesenza" Father Russo writes as follows: "Archbishop Nogara was a Shepherd solely devoted to the care of souls. The inscription on his coat of arms read: "Volentem duco, nolentem traho," "The willing ones I lead—the reluctant I charm." Like St. Paul, he was a restless worker for the Kingdom of God and his only rest was to change from one activity to a different one. He spoke very quickly and, like St. Paul, he mentioned the Name of Jesus to no end in his sermons. He was decidedly upright to the point of looking rather stern and rigid; but he had a great heart, quite ready to grasp the situation, incapable of duplicity and most sympathetic for the needs of souls, of the clergy and of the times. In the course of pastoral visitations, quite a few times he had nothing to eat until he returned very tired to the Bishop's House late at night, because he didn't want to add a new burden to the meagre budget of some pastors. Oh, how many fine and large Parish Rectories he established in his Diocese."

Archbishop Nogara left his image deeply impressed on the hearts of the junior cosentine clergy for whose welfare he ever displayed a fatherly concern. Universal was the grief felt for his premature death. The Archdiocese had gradually resumed the dynamic course of better days. Pastoral action was inspired by the wise directives and by the example of the tireless Shepherd. An exemplary life, completely dedicated to the welfare of souls, capable of perfect detachment, because of its spirit of faith and sacrifice, is like the flag that gives new strength and courage to the soldier on the battlefield.

"Now I have something to tell your elders: I,—writes St. Peter —who am an elder myself and a witness to the sufferings of Christ, and with you I have a share in the glory that is to be revealed. Be the shepherds of the flock of God that is entrusted to you: watch over it, not simply as a duty but gladly, because God wants it: not for sordid money, but because you are eager to do it. Never be a dictator over any group that is put in your charge, but be an example that the whole flock can follow." (I Pt. 5, 1-4)

His Excellency Archbishop Nogara was quickly informed

concerning the situation in the Archdiocese and the good accomplished by Sister Elena. Canon Saverio Mazzuca gave him an exact description of the extraordinary events that had occurred, as usual, during the Fridays in Lent of that year up to Good Friday. He felt esteem and predilection for Sister Elena's work as is attested by the following letter.

Cosenza, Holy Thursday
The Archbishop of Cosenza

To Reverend Sister Elena Aiello
Cosenza.

Knowing as I do, the truly holy work to which you have consecrated your whole life by sheltering and educating in a motherly way so many poor little girls, that are abandoned and exposed to danger, I deem it my duty to express my utmost gratitude to you and to assure you as well of my personal interest in the development of such a deserving institution that is so well appreciated by our fellow citizens.

I feel I should make this known to you in a very special way in order to put an end to chatter and to wicked insinuations whose purpose is to instigate suspicion and to cast aspersion on your labors which are solely fostered by the holiest feelings of christian charity. I believe that this tribute by your Archbishop shall not only insure and even increase the good will of your followers and benefactors, but that it shall also bring you some consolation and reward—in part at least—for all your sufferings thus far. I said "in part at least" for I am sure you are not expecting a recompense from men but rather from the One God, the Just Remunerator of the bit of good we are able to do here below.

With my special blessing to You, to Your Sisters and to Your little girls, I am

Sincerely,
Robert Nogara, *Archbishop*

The painful trials, alluded to by the Archbishop, had started a year or so before. In 1933, during the Holy Year commemorating the Redemption, the extraordinary phenomenon recurred with greater intensity.

During that time some people succeeded in getting to Elena's room with the intention of discovering some element suitable to

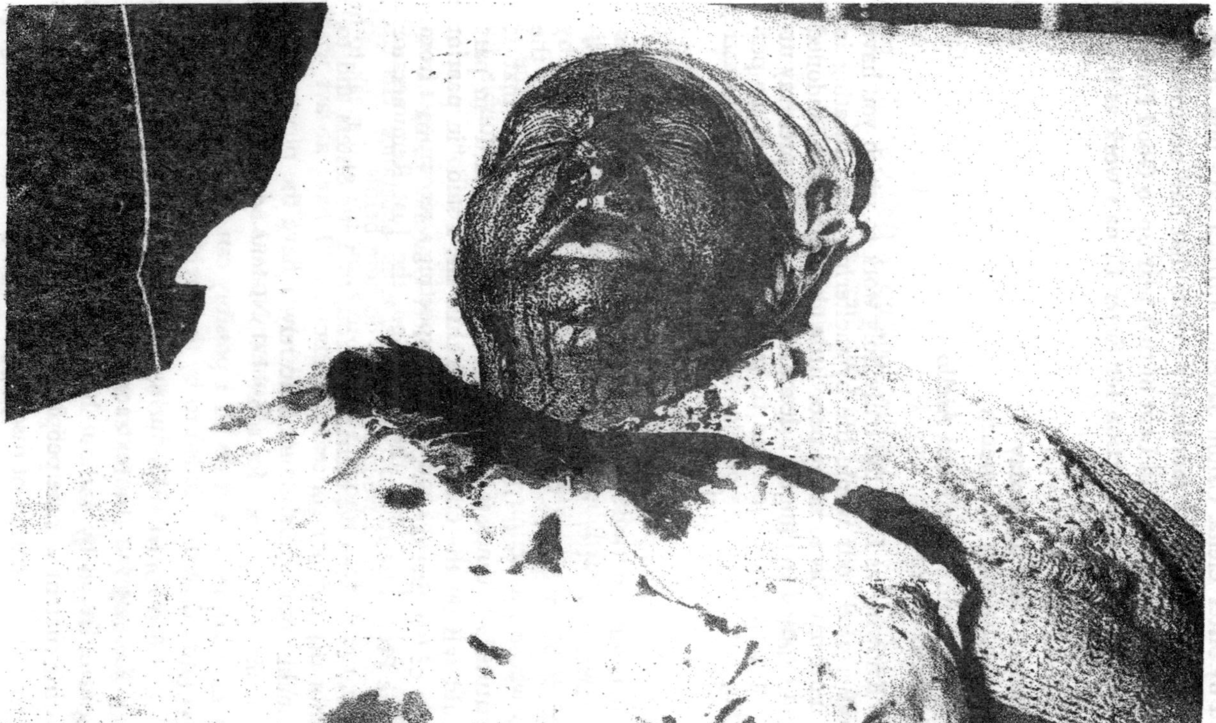

Sister Elena Aiello During the Phenomenon of Her Suffering. Good Friday, 2:40 p.m., 1959.

him retract from that same pulpit all he had so thoughtlessly said.

Brother Avemaria, Don Orione's blind hermit, who lived in solitude, prayer and penance in the mountain monastery of Sant'Alberto di Butrio, surrounded by the chestnut trees of Val Staffora, used to say to despondent people: "Remember that man was not created to be the absolute master of his own destiny. He was created by God Who wants to be his Father, so that man may live in His divine family. Woe to anyone presuming to be self-sufficient, able to clear up all his problems. God wants to share our life. He is always close to us and it is He Who directs our life along the right way. Everybody should be warned not to resist God. They should rather look up to God with filial confidence after having calmly done all they could."

This boundless confidence explains Sister Elena's composure in her daily work for the little ones and for the entire Community, as well as her vigorous impulse for the greater expansion of the Institute. She sought help from benevolent persons, begged of her creditors to be patient and understanding, but, above all, she looked up to Divine Providence and ever guided her little orphan girls to God's Altar. For a little while she also sent to benefactors a letter containing two small pictures, one of St. Francis of Paola and the other of St. Teresa of the Infant Jesus "to whose protection is entrusted the First House of the New Institute." At times, if pressed with a more serious trouble, Elena would call on the City Prefecture. In the notebook mention is made of her first meeting with Prefect Giacone. Elena had gone to the Prefecture in order to request some assistance. His Excellency, the Prefect, who had wished to know her and speak to her personally did not conceal his emotion. "I have always wished to make your acquaintance, and now I have the pleasure to see you come to my office for some help. I find no words to express my satisfaction. I shall do all I possibly can to help you in your charitable work."

As a first contribution, he set aside 10 kilograms of bread for each day and 250 lire for each month. Besides, he never let an opportunity go by without helping the Institute. One day the electric current was shut off because of non-payment of a bill that was overdue. The result? Darkness for the whole evening. After asking God's help, Elena walked to the Company's office and begged for their consideration and cooperation. The Director immediately issued an order to have the current restored and prescribed that, henceforth, Sister Elena "was not to be disturbed" when unable to pay. Most remarkable was the way plain working people were also willing to help. For example, sometimes they would buy and deliver to Sister Elena's orphan girls some of those large loaves of bread that were baked in Donnici and sold at the County Seat. However, much more than that was needed to strike a balance between the daily heavy expenditures and the intermittent meagre donations that, at most, could overcome only some of the eventual difficulties.

That evident disproportion gives us a glimpse of the action of Divine Providence which never failed to take care of what was needed even by means of extraordinary interventions. On September 11, 1935, when Sister Gigia and her brothers had left for Bucita, Sister Elena spent a painful night. It so happened that there was no food on hand in the kitchen for the noon meal. Sister Angela asked her Superior for some money. In the meantime a Priest came in, requested to say Mass and walked to the Sacristy right away. Not having anything on hand, Sister Elena told Sister Angela to first go and hear Mass and then somehow the Lord would provide. Elena's prayer in union with that of the Sisters and of the orphan girls, was quickly heard. For right after the Elevation, a strong fragrance spread through the Chapel.

Sister Elena was at the time reciting the Office of the Blessed Virgin from the second page of her prayer book. Suddenly she spotted a 50 lire bill between the prayer card of Our Lady of Sorrows and that of St. Teresa. She was positive that nothing of the kind had previously been in her prayer book as she had recited the very same prayer, on that very same page, on the previous evening.

Anyway, after Mass and after handing the 50 lire bill for the day's needs, Sister Elena with all the girls went back to the Chapel, and there within earshot, she prayed to God to let her find another 50 lire in her prayer book at the same place as an unquestionable proof that the first 50 lire had not been forgotten by someone, but that they were actually the gift of Divine Providence. During the day, some of the bigger girls and even one or two of the Sisters went searching through that prayer book which had been left at its place. In the evening, when the Community assembled in the Chapel for the evening prayers, while the "Confiteor" was being recited, the same kind of a fragrance as in the morning was felt. Elena got greatly excited. She didn't dare open her prayer book, but passed it on to Sister Teresa to do so. Sister obeyed and there were the additional 50 lire between the two prayer cards, at the same place. In the white circle there was a green handwriting, 50 + 50 = 100 with some letters of the Greek alphabet.

The following morning Elena related the incident to her Confessor, Canon Mazzuca, who insisted on looking at the 50 lire banknotes—No. 01670 and 0039. However, the inscription on the white circle had completely disappeared. Father Benjamin Mazza, who wished to retain those banknotes, exchanged them with one for 100 lire. That one is now in our possession.

In 1934, on the vigil of St. Joseph, a payment was due to Pietro Rizzo of Montalto for a quintal of oil. Sister Elena gathered her orphan girls around the Altar and prayed with them to that great saint, the Head of the Holy Family. Toward evening a benefactor came to the Institute and gave a donation corresponding exactly to the sum due on that quintal of oil.

On another day in 1937, bread was needed in the present Institute headquarters. The Sister, who had asked for money to buy it, was told to request the baker to give it on credit. However, since that credit had been on the books for a long time, she didn't have the courage to do so, and naturally came home empty-handed. At mealtime after saying the usual prayers, Elena noticing that there was no bread on hand, offered a mental prayer to God. That very moment a municipal guard knocked at the door of the Institute and delivered 36 kilograms of bread which had been picked up as a result of a violation that very morning.

On another occasion Sister Elena saw some of her little orphans coming to her with the story that 'pasta" was the only food in the kitchen. Sister Elena caressed them and led them to the Chapel saying: "Just pray and you will see that God will provide." Within a few minutes Elena was sent for because the City Questor had just brought in 18 kilograms of fish. That officer was frankly amazed when he heard from Elena what we have just related, and he was all the more amazed when, on entering the Chapel, he saw for himself the little girls still fervently praying.

In 1938 Sister Angela greeted a gentleman who, after visiting the Institute, left a donation of 5,000 lire. The Sister couldn't conceal her excitement, because, as she told the Benefactor, that very day, the baker had discontinued delivering bread to the Institute because their debt had reached the sum of 5,000 lire. As previously at Montalto, so now here also, quite a few people called on Elena whenever the dying refused the Sacraments. Besides praying for them, she would hasten to their bedside. Take the case of Antonio, a cabinet maker, who had been leading a disreputable life. As he lay dying with a smoker's cancer, he wouldn't permit anyone to see him. His mother confided her problem to Sister Elena who went there that same evening. She had taken along some tangerines and, on entering, she said she had come just to greet him and to ascertain how he was faring. The sick man rejoiced at that unexpected visit. Sister Elena remained there a long time, inquiring about his illness, coaxing him to drink some sugared water, cheering him and thus gaining his confidence. She assured him she was willing to return, provided he would be willing to receive the Sacraments. He consented wholeheartedly and asked for the Superior of the Minims. Sister Elena pleased him at once. That same evening the Superior heard his confession and gave him Holy Communion. After midnight the sick man lost consciousness, but he came to at noon, and asked for Extreme Unction. The Sacrament was administered by the Superior of the Minims and shortly after, the sick man, with Elena praying for him, breathed his last. I shall now mention only one other such case. The members of a certain family hardly ever practiced their religious duties. Since she knew it, Elena urged the Rector of St. Francesco's Church to present them with a little framed picture of the Saint when making the house to house collection for the impending feast. While the collection was actually taking place, Sister Elena dreamt that Mr. N., a member of that family, had committed suicide. In the morning Sister Elena informed the Superior of the Minims about that dream and urged him to call on that family. It was about noon. As he left the Institute, Father Superior went straight to the resident of S., taking Giulio Domma with him. They were climbing the stairs when they heard a loud, double gun explosion. Rushing into the room with Major Alberto, a son of Mr. N., they saw that the unfortunate man had shot himself through the mouth with his hunting gun. The lower jaw had been almost completely shattered and part of the upper one had been ripped up to the eye. The suicide told the superior that he had acted thus in a moment of temporary despondency and that he was sorry for his crime. That being so, he asked Don Antonio Del Vecchio, the Cathedral's Rector, to hear his confession, and to administer all the other sacraments which he humbly received.

CHAPTER TEN

Foretelling the Passing of an Archbishop

ON THE OCCASION of the First General Chapter, in November 1956, a detailed report was submitted concerning the functions and the disciplinary and individual requirements of the Institute. In that report, which is an official document, mention is made of the work accomplished at the House on Revocati Street (1928). "After happily achieving our cherished goal, we decided to assemble about one hundred children for our nursery. At the same time the Archbishop exhorted us to teach the catechism in the Church del Rito of Panebianco as well as in St. Giovanni's Church. We also took care of those who had not received Holy Communion at an early stage and assisted the dying as well."

"We stayed at No. 11 Revocati Street for over one year, after which we moved to the Caselli property where the quarters were quite large and suitable for the development of our work. In fact, besides the kindergarten, we were able to open an after school class, an embroidery and sewing room for the local girls and a supervised recreational Center."

"The report goes on: 'On December 4, 1929, I requested to have a Mass said in the Church of St. Francis of Assisi by Father Giovanni Corrao, the Pastor. Our intention was to get a clear idea of the kind of work we should engage in and also to expect some definite sign by midday. Representing the Archbishop, Monsignor Sironi called here at noon in company with Mr. Giovanni Zeni, holding in one hand a picture of his late wife, and with the other, a little orphan girl by the name of Rita from Portopiana. He desired to give her a home in memory of his late wife and for this purpose he was pledging 50 lire monthly, a diamond pin, etc. From the 4th to the 18th of December six more girls were admitted. Blessed by God and encouraged by Archbishop Trussoni, that kind of work met with the approval of the Cosentine people who never failed to foster and support it with every kind of assistance and protection.'"

"A brief reference is made here concerning the transfer to the Rural Bank old quarters, located in the Holy Spirit district, where 60 girls were housed. The particular benevolence of the following Prefects is gratefully acknowledged: Bianchetti, Giacone, La Russa, Palmardita, Bellini, Arinolfo, Endrise: (from 1942 on) Adami, Marfisa, Lo Monaco and all the other Provincial Authorities. The painstaking cooperation of Mother Vicar's Brothers is also emphasized. "The Rev. Mazza Fathers have been our true guardian angels; they have followed our work step by step from the very beginning; they have guided and edified us in all our trials. We shall never forget all the good that they, as God's ministers, have done to our souls as well as for their family's material assistance to us."

Their work for the welfare of the orphan girls is described in the following way: "The little seed yielded abundant fruit, Divine Providence never failed to take care of our needs. We were able to look after the girls' spiritual and temporal welfare, to make them fit for the social and family life, and make them skillful in sewing, designing and knitting. It was imperative for the orphan girls to complete the entire Grammar School course. These little girls are allowed to stay in the Institute until they are 22 years old. Under no circumstances are they to be given away as servant girls but solely for adoption or marriage. Otherwise they shall remain in our Community, since that is the specific object of our Institute."

"At the time we resided in the Holy Spirit district, the following were adopted as daughters: Franceschina Chioda, Iolanda Biance, Maria Gallo, Mariantonia Torchio." The report then dwells on the purpose of the present Generalate House. "During the four years that we lived in the above named district the number of the Sisters and of the little orphans increased steadily. Hence, Elena dreamed of a much bigger house with a garden, if possible. Opposite our balconies (on the other side of the river) one could see the profile of a rugged building with an adjacent big garden. It was a nice, isolated property. The Ferri family that resided in Bologna intended to use it as a private residence, but they had left is unfinished. To us it looked like a dream, like a dream that could never be fulfilled. However, I felt within me an urge to pray and to make the little ones pray, because nothing is impossible to God. The Lord heard our insistent prayers. During the summer of 1935 we talked it over with the brothers of Mother Vicar and with Counsellor Francesco Cribari, a very dear friend of the Institute. After looking over both the building and the extensive grounds, they resolved to purchase it at once. Counsellor Cribari left for Bologna and, through the cosentine Guiseppe D'Andrea, Inspector General of the Secret Police, was able to induce Giacomo Ferri, nephew of Senator Giacomo, to release the house and attached grounds for the sum of 165,000 lire."

Archbishop Nogara was very much in favor of that purchase, in fact, he was enthused about that big house and its healthy location. Moreover, he assured us that, as soon as we would get the deed to the property, he would manage to have his nephew, Aldisio, Director General of the Banca del Lavoro, make arrangements for a loan. That property was a gift of Senator Ferri to his little nephew Giacomino, who resided in Bologna, and who, later on, decided to sell it. Quite a few persons had tried to get it, as, for instance, the Nun C., who, however, had declined to take it at the price of 100,000 lire. At Sister Elena's request, Sister Gigia hastened to call on the legal administrator, who being well informed of the poverty of the two Nuns, asked point blank: "Have you any money?" "Of course not," was the reply. "Well, in that case," the lawyer answered, "you can have the Ferri property, if you still want it, for 149,000 lire." We have just seen how Counsellor Cribari had gone all the way to Bologna to deal directly with the Ferris'. The contract was stipulated at Cosenza on June 29, 1936. On the previous evening Elena had returned home quite exhausted, for she had walked to and fro in an effort to pick up the money needed for the following day, but to no avail. Late in the evening she was saying the Rosary in the parlor, facing a large picture of the Sacred Heart of Jesus. At a certain moment, stung by pain torturing her bleeding feet, she cried out, "O Lord, have mercy on me! Aren't you appeased with the nails piercing your feet? Please help us!" At that very moment a shattering sound was heard, as if the glass on the picture had been broken in pieces. So loud was the noise that Sister Gigia who had retired, quite worried, got up and turned on the light; but there was no breakage anywhere. They believed that the sound was a sign that the Lord would come to their assistance. As a matter of fact, in the morning, when Sister Elena sought Counsellor Cribari's advice on how to get the money for that contract, Francesco Goffredo, the notary public, telephoned Mr. Cribari to call right away because he would advance the money if Sister Elena didn't have the correct amount. While the two Nuns were on their way to sign the contract, Chevalier Piro gave them the 10 lire for the purchase of the legal paper.

Mr. Goffredo, the Notary Public, advanced the first 14,000 lire for the contract fees, since Sister Elena had only 1,000 lire which was a loan from Francesco Florio. The building had to be completed so as to make it ready for occupancy. Since Archbishop Nogara had counselled to complete the building at a low cost, Master Vincenzo Lagana—a brother-in-law of Mother Vicar, and a man who could be trusted—was summoned to Cosenza. His job was to organize whatever was needed for the completion of the building and of the surrounding sheds. About twenty working men, and quite a few Cosenza firms, were employed in that connection. Mancuso, Cipparrone, Pignitore, loaned the material without any binding clause. A bank book for 5,000 lire donated by Rev. Filippo Nigro, Pastor of Zumbano, was the first offering to that house. The aforementioned Pastor had successfully retrieved his deposit from an insolvent bank through the kindness of Prefect Palmardita and of the Director of the Banca d'Italia. The project was finished in about one year at a cost of 170,000 lire. Divine Providence saw to it that enough donations and supplies came in each time for the settlement of all the expenditures.

During the summer of 1937, one section of the Community

came to occupy the new quarters, but Sister Elena insisted on waiting until the Chapel was ready because she intended to move there together with our Eucharistic Lord. At last the solemn dedication was held in the presence of Church and Lay Dignitaries. Foremost among them and beaming with pleasure were Archbishop Nogara and Prefect Palmardita. We continue quoting from the report.

"During the period between 1937 and 1942 the group of the little girls totalled 80: that of the Nuns: 52, of which 22 were professed, 14 were Novices and 16 aspirants. Fourteen of them were graduate designers and seamstresses: 4 had won diplomas in knitting and 6 in embroidery. During that same year the first vocations flourished among the abandoned girls, i.e., Sister Angela Trotta (the present Mother General and Superior of the Montalto House from the very beginning) and Sister Veronica.

"In 1940 the Professional Department for Technical Instruction earned the State approval and enabled us to exhibit our products at the first showing in the presence of Honorable Bottai. We were awarded four knitting machines and 5,000 lire." At this point, after briefly recalling the opposition and the jealousy of some people, the letter of His Excellency Nogara previously reported is quoted in full. Then it goes on: "In 1941, four of our Sisters undertook the Kindergarten Teaching Course and in 1942 they graduated in Rome at Father Giovanni Semeria's Master Institute and Method School. On February 24, 1942, five Novices made their Profession and fourteen Postulants received their habit. On July 10, 1942, at 10:30, His Holiness Pope Pius XII received in private audience, Mother Vicar, four of our Sisters, and myself. His Holiness inquired about the number of our Sisters, the specific object of the Institute and on what kind of resources we depended for our support. As I replied that the Institute depended on charity of benefactors, the Pope beaming with pleasure said: "My daughters do not worry. I assure you that your work will expand because it is based on Divine Providence!" What a blessed prophecy and how perfectly fulfilled! For our Institute thenceforth kept steadily moving forward.

The war and the invasion in 1943 caused us to cancel the

reception of new candidates. Being refugees at Montalto, we too had suffered heavy losses on account of war bombardments. For that reason the Novices couldn't make their profession and eight postulants were unable to receive the habit. However, in 1946, we quickly resumed our activities by accepting new Postulants. Thirteen of them received the habit in 1947, and they took temporary vows in 1948. Then in 1949 it was the first time that twenty-five of our Sisters took perpetual vows. Forty-two additional Sisters took temporary vows from 1949 to 1955 inclusive. Eight other Postulants were admitted to the Novitiate in 1956 and twenty-two Sisters professed perpetual vows. Our work had been placed under the powerful protection of St. Francis of Paola —that great Saint of Charity—for whom we ever entertained a special devotion. In order to follow a safe rule of religious life we have been guided more by the spirit than by the Rule of St. Francis of Paola. Later on I took care to write a rule to which I gradually added some pious practices and regulations, the better to fulfil the specific scope of our Institute.

"On April 21, 1944, the General Council was convoked with Sister Elena Aiello as Mother General, Sister Gigia Mazza as Mother Vicar. Three Sisters of the older group were chosen as their assistants, i.e., Sister Carmelina Cribari, Sister Teresa Infusino, and Sister Angela Padula. The Institute has been functioning with growing vigor and discipline; yet its religious spirit was never wanting.

"All possible attention was given to the spiritual formation of candidates. Spiritual Retreats have been held each year, as well as the monthly retreat conducted by the Very Reverend Francesco Mazza of the Minims. All the Sisters were able to attend them. Later on, when Father Mazza was transferred to Palermo as Superior, he was replaced by the Reverend don Aniello Calcara, and the Very Reverend Father Sarago of the Minims was appointed as Spiritual Director.

"After returning from Palermo, the Very Reverend Father Mazza was elected Provincial because of the explicit desire of Father Francesco Sarago who had been transferred to Rome. Resuming his work Father Mazza has been conducting the monthly Retreat since 1946, whereas Father Vincenzo Donnarumma, who had come back to Cosenza in the role of Superior, was appointed as Spiritual Director."

Alas, in April 1940, the Archdiocese of Cosenza was bereft of its Shepherd by a premature death. "In September 1939, Sister Elena confided to me: About this time next year, His Excellency shall no longer be in Cosenza." I didn't question her any further, neither did I pay any attention to the meaning of those words. On one of my frequent visits to His Excellency, I related the Sister's remarks. In my excitement I had believed, that, since the Archbishop was Administrator of Reggio Calabria, he might be promoted to that Archdiocese, the more so, because up to that time he enjoyed perfect health.

The following day, when I said that I had quoted her words to His Excellency as alluding to a promotion to Reggio Calabria, Sister Elena became visibly depressed; then in her usually simple way, she hinted that such was not the case. The first symptoms of a severe illness became apparent in November. His Excellency felt happy for having somehow cooperated to the Beautification of Gemma Galgani. The two miracles which had been discussed and approved for that occasion, had been wrought in the Cosenza Archdiocese, and he had enlisted his dynamic energy for the promotion of that cause. He was hoping that Gemma would cure him. However, Our Lord had disposed otherwise. When the operation was decided on, it was too late and it was no longer possible. Sister Elena hastened to visit the Archbishop as he, perfectly conscious, was awaiting the very end.

She told me, that, as soon as she entered the room, she saw the Archbishop's sister, Mother Giulia, Superior of the Sister Adorers in Garda, on one side of the bed and Gemma Galgani on the other. Before expiring His Excellency told Mother Giulia that the only thing he would have very much desired was the approbation and juridical recognition of the Institute. With Archbishop Nogara's passing, a long period of spiritual misery, besides physical suffering, began very soon for Sister Elena and her Institute. With the exception of some brief interruptions, it became her normal way of life.

Pretty soon the fatherly benevolence and enlightened understanding of His Excellency Trussoni, the protection and earnest concern of His Excellency Nogara who was a tower of strength for the Institute, a support and solace in trials for Sister Elena, gave way to misunderstanding, mistrust, frequent deeds and expressions that, independently of the intention, caused pain and humiliations to the Foundress, to the Sisters and to her Institute.

The Institute was already firmly established when the Archbishop died: it was flourishing to such a point that its sturdy roots, if checked at one point, would vigorously sprout somewhere else. Now it was ready for even greater expansion under the extraordinary impulse of that suffering, yet dynamic woman —who was to spread a work blessed by God, and to extend it through her Sisters in the Cosenza Archdiocese, elsewhere and even as far away as Rome. Thus, the Institution that had its origin in 1928, achieved its climax during the period of 1940-1961 because of the juridical recognition by the Holy See.

CHAPTER ELEVEN

Unceasing Labor Under Trials

EIGHTEEN ARE THE HOUSES established by Sister Elena. Moreover, the Sisters opened also a House at Pentone (Catanzaro) on February 10, 1952, at the insistent request of the Pastor, and they retained it for several years. It consisted of a kindergarten, and a workroom for cut work, sewing and embroidery. For some time they worked also at Pietrapaola in the Rossano Archdiocese, but they left on August 31, 1953. Following the custom of the Mother House, the Sisters besides fulfilling the specific activity of the Congregation, always attended to Catechetical instructions, to Catholic Action and to the Children's Mass. Each House has its own particular story to tell. Indeed for the establishment of some of them, Sister Elena had a hard fight on her hands, so much so that on two occasions—particularly for St. Sisto—the Sacred Congregation of the Religious had to directly intervene in her favor.

Moreover, she had to overcome other kinds of obstacles as a result of endless bureaucratic practices. The report read in the Second General Chapter of 1961, which was held right after Sister Elena's death, adds some other particulars. We are told of the Novitiate, a new building adjoining the Mother House. Mention is made of the Home for the Aged at S. Fili donated by the kind-hearted brothers Carlo and Emma Manes and of the request made by Bishop Barberi of Cassano Ionio in 1958 to have Sisters serve at the Mormanno Seminary during the summer months. We are also told of the purchase of the house made on Baldassini Street by Sister Elena who had purposely come to Rome with Sister Imelda Mazzulla and Sister Francesca Lopez in November 29, 1957. The report then deals with Montalto Uffugo and with the House at Cosenza—S. Vito.

"In 1958 the old building of the Institute St. Rita of Cascia in Montalto had to be rebuilt because some of its walls were in danger of collapsing. Due to the shrewd and feverish activity of Mother Foundress we were able to receive from the Ministry of Public Works the first quota of twelve million lire in June 1959 and, with the cooperation of the Catanzaro Corps of Engineers, we started the demolition and then the reconstruction work. The building was completed in about three years at a total cost of 83 million lire. From its lofty elevation it looks quite impressive and, its panoramic view is truly enchanting. It consists of two stories and a basement with 36 large rooms and Chapel, all large enough to satisfy the needs of about 100 students. One large wing of that building serves as the Grammar, the Intermediate, and the Teachers Training Schools. The Intermediate received State approval years ago, and the Teachers' Training was finally accredited in 1960. Sister Elena realized at once their importance and usefulness for the young congregation. Hence, she spared no expenses and left no stone unturned to get their juridical recognition. Monsignor Umberto Cameli of the Sacred Congregation of the Universities and Seminaries aided her very much by his counsel and guidance. Both Schools represent today a solid institution that is very much appreciated in the City, in the Province, and elsewhere. Owing to the Teachers' cultural preparation and to the tireless activity of the Superior, Sister Angela Trotta (now Mother General) the School has been very profitable to the Community in as much as it has enabled some of the Sisters to get a Teacher's Diploma and others to be on the staff of the Teachers' Faculty. Two of the Sisters, having already graduated, are now teaching at the Montalto School; another is about to graduate: four of them are teaching in the grammar school and ten others are qualified to teach in the preparatory school."

The Cosenza House in S. Vito district became an actual fact on October 1, 1960; it was built on a plot donated by Baron Mollo. It looks like a dream. It doesn't seem possible, yet our good Mother launched that building operation when she had only 15,000 lire on hand. The project was completed by many donations and by free labor provided by several construction companies. The Institute dedicated to the Immaculate Heart of Mary Mediatrix of all graces between men and God, is now boarding 50 children of the ENAOLI.

We have already alluded to the officious antagonism that prevailed at the time of Archbishop Nogara's death. Our Lord was permitting it in order—I would say—to make it crystal clear that the project and its expansion were truly the work of Divine Providence. As God's way is to act forcefully, yet sweetly, achieving His ends by the use of the most unusual means, so it was concerning Elena and her Institute. For, if He permitted misunderstanding and antagonism on one side, He also saw to it that, besides the ever increasing army of even prominent benefactors, other persons should arise showing benevolent interest in her projects and willing to help her overcome any obstacle to her work.

The first place belongs to the late beloved Monsignor Roberto Sposetti, an expert Assistant, up to 1953, to the Congregation of the Religious. Then we recall the two Very Rev. Father Assistants, Giuseppe Manzo, S.J., (1949-1952) a former Provincial in Naples, and Bonaventura de Pavullo, Pontifical Assistant of the Institute from 1952 to this day. We have previously mentioned the Very Reverend Father Francesco Sarago.

We must now call attention to a Priest to whom we owe a great deal of information from 1937 on. He has kindly placed at our disposal a set of informative papers and about one hundred personal letters. That is the voice of a witness, for he was able, from 1935 on, to follow the series of events that we are trying to outline in this preliminary study. We shall simply call him don Franco, for so he was addressed by the Mother General. He readily exhibits documents that we now submit to prove our point. There was a lot of work to be done for the completion of S. Sisto's house from January 1951 to March 5, 1952.

On May 29, 1951, Sister Elena wrote to Father Manzo as follows: "As I have already informed you about S. Sisto's house, it was since last January that I asked and obtained permission from

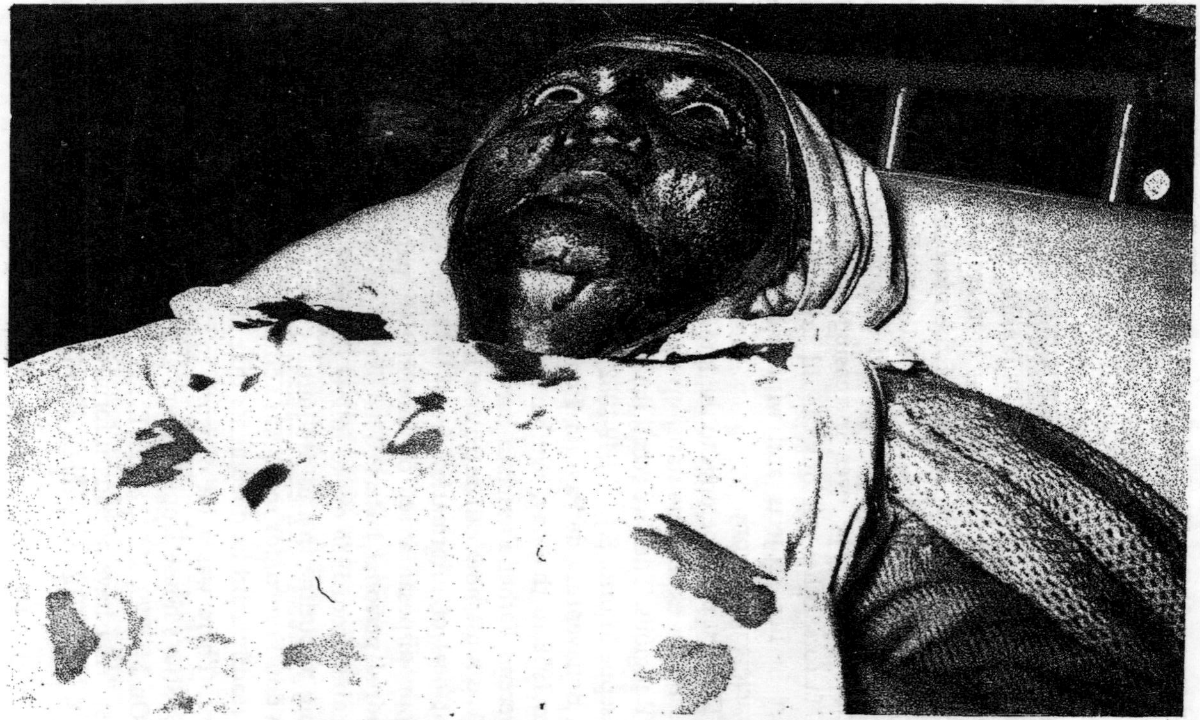

Sister Elena Aiello in Agony, Good Friday, 3:00 p.m., 1961.

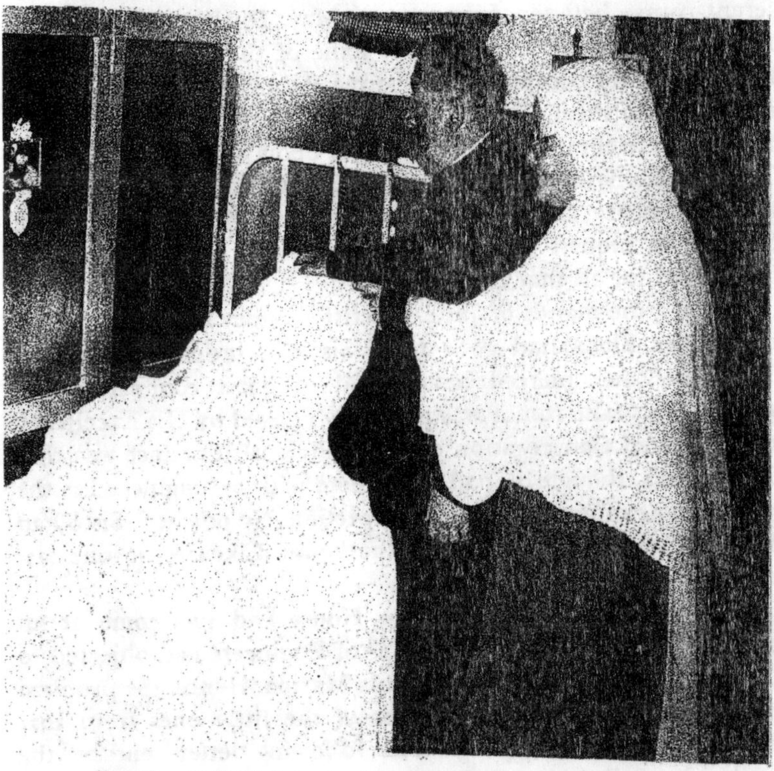

Sister Elena Aiello Pointing to Jesus' Face While Monsignor Cioffi Looks on.

the Archbishop through the Very Reverend Father Sarago, Assistant General of the Minims, who was passing through Cosenza, to take possession of our benefactors' bequest and to attend to the opening of the house they had donated to our Institute."

A similar statement was made by her on July 21, 1951, in a letter to the Prefect of Cosenza who had forbidden the summer camp already prepared at S. Sisto, on account of Ecclesiastical disapproval. As a matter of fact, the situation had taken a different course between January and May. During the month of May, when Mother General sent some of the Sisters to get the house ready for occupancy, the young Pastor openly declared his opposition to them. To prevent them from attending Holy Mass, he began celebrating behind closed doors except on Sunday. The parishioners turned against him. When a request was made to the Cosenza Carabineers to have the Minim Sisters leave S. Sisto, an inquest brought out the fact that the Pastor was to be blamed for all that trouble.

During the month of June, a fictitious story made the rounds that Sister Elena had gone to S. Sisto in order to show her "stigmata," her pierced hands, and to boast concerning her visions. This false rumor was promptly relayed by His Excellency to the Sacred Congregation of the Religious! The fact was that Sister Elena, though ill, had gone there with an engineer for the sole purpose of making a house inspection. No one at S. Sisto had seen her leave the car, or enter the house. Likewise no one saw her leaving after the inspection.

The donation of the S. Sisto House had just come at an opportune time, because the Corps of Engineers had objected to the occupancy of the House at Paola Marina. Hence, the problem had to be solved for the transfer of the little ones from that house to some other place. The following letter sent by the Archbishop's Delegate and dated June 16, 1951, makes explicit reference to that matter.

Very Reverend Sister Elena Aiello
Cosenza.

In reply to your two letters, I wish you to know that we are perfectly aware of having mailed you two letters on two separate occasions, i.e., on the 24th and on the 26th of last May. You have been explicitly forbidden to open a religious house at S. Sisto dei Valdesi. You were told to make some other arrangements for the little girls of Paola either in some of your houses or elsewhere. Hence, we cannot but remind you of your duty to obey explicit orders.

Greetings,

THE DELEGATE

At last, after a few months, owing to Father Manzo's resolute attitude, His Excellency stated that he would remove the Pastor and grant permission to the Sisters to stay at S. Sisto on the one condition that Mother General would sign the document enclosed in his letter, admitting it was all her fault. In obedience to Father Manzo, who, as Religious Assistant to the Institute, advised her to sign, Mother General had some other Nun affix her signature. She notified Father Manzo with her usual candor by a letter in which her very soul seems to be throbbing, as if wounded, on account of her love for truth and justice.

The following letter brought the case to a close.

To the Superior General of the Minim Sisters
Cosenza

March 5, 1952.

Since you mailed me your praiseworthy letter in which you reaffirm your intention to practice prompt and submissive obedience, and since I have been able to restore order in S. Sisto Parish, by the appointment of a new Pastor, I wholeheartedly grant you permission to open your house in that town and to staff it with Sisters without delay. Of course it will be your duty to first notify the Pastor. I follow you with my pastoral blessing in order that in a spirit of humble obedience to the Pastor, you may do fine and fruitful work for the salvation of souls and for God's glory. You have my fatherly blessing in Christ.

During that same year (1951) the opening of a kindergarten in a small village of the Tropea Diocese failed to go through because, according to a statement by the Redemptorist Father Oreste De Simone to the Mother General (November 15, 1951) the references given by His Excellency the Archbishop, were not satisfactory. The very same thing happened to the house at Lago (Cosenza).

By his last will and testament, arranged by Notary Public Counsellor Luigi Goffredo on February 13, 1952, and made public June 5, 1953, Michele Adamo bequeathed his "Health Lodging House" to Sister Elena for the benefit of the orphan girls.

Mother General forwarded a copy of the testament to the Archbishop begging him to permit the opening of that Orphanage according to the testator's will (July 6, 1953). His Excellency graciously granted that request with the following letter:

To the Very Reverend Sister Elena
Cosenza

Having made preliminary inquiries, we gladly give you permission to open a house in Lafo Parish, as requested by you on July 6, 1953, to be used as an orphanage for little girls. Concerning parish activities, your Sisters shall engage only in those requested by the Pastor in order to insure both coordination and systematic function.

For the "House Opening" please make the necessary arrangements with the Very Reverend Pastor D. Federico Faraco, to whom you are to submit a copy of this letter.

My fatherly blessing to you.

The "Nulla Osta" by the Sacred Congregation of the Religious for the acceptance of the Adamo bequest came through on August 17, 1955. The Very Reverend Father Assistant and Mother Vicar went to Lago and reached complete agreement with the Pastor. The sole difficulty to that transaction was the actual presence of tenants who were enjoying the benefit of rent control.

Now, while we were marking time for the tenants to vacate, the late testator's sister, with the Archbishop's consent, removed the tenants and, in agreement with the Pastor, placed in our house in December 1964, an ex-Franciscan Nun with five elderly people. And so we got nowhere. From Rome, don Franco sent the following letter to His Excellency Calcara on September 22, 1956, on behalf of the two orphanages at Carolei and at S. Fili.

Your Excellency:

I heard today from Monsignor Carol of the Secretariat that a mutual agreement has been reached with Your Excellency for the assignment of the Sister Minims to the new orphanage that was inaugurated yesterday at Carolei. However, Your Excellency's preference for the S. Fili orphanage is apparently for the Sisters of Divine Providence. I was shocked and grieved for such exclusion of the Sister Minims from S. Fili where they have been staying for a number of years. For, from the several talks we had on this matter for the past few months, I had the impression that Your Excellency had been graciously considering the appointment of the Sister Minims for both Orphanages. Now by the very fact of their elimination, an unfavorable judgment will naturally affect that young Congregation. May I be permitted to earnestly beg Your Excellency to kindly spare the Sister Minims this new humiliation.

Your humble servant,

The following was his reply.

Cosenza, September 28, 1956

Reverend Professor:

I am interested only up to a certain point about the judgment of the Carolei Pastor who wishes to have the Minims for the supervision of the "Boys Home" and the judgment of the S. Fili Pastor who doesn't want them. for it is up to me to make a decision.

It is just for this reason that I am waiting for an answer from Monsignor Carol's office. In the meantime it is important for you to take a definite stand in order to prevent equivocations which inconvenience everybody and may cause harm rather than good to the Minim's Institute. Since the Sacred Congregation of the Religious has clarified the juridical status of that Institute, as being of Diocesan right, the Archbishop is its Protector, as he has been in the past. Therefore, both you, and someone else along with you, have to stop pretending you are protectors of the above mentioned Institute. For, the obvious impression on the part of those who are concerned, is that you are doing so in order to pro tect the Minims—strange to say—from the Archbishop . . . as is apparent from some reports written by people who know to draft them.

Once and for all let us put a stop to this foolish word play and let the Minims replace their unconditional faith in their Archbishop. This faith should never be wanting, even if, at times, he will have to decide contrary to their judgment or desires. That may happen and it does happen in some circumstances, in order to test both the virtue and the spirit of obedience which is the foundation of spiritual perfection. You are intelligent enough to understand that what I have suggested is the only way to help your dear Institute move forward. As I am confident you will do so, I wholeheartedly bless you.

A. CALCARA, *Archbishop*

P.S. Please prevail upon the Sister Minims to come directly to me, as all the other Nuns are doing both for what concerns the Boys' Home and for any other matter they have at heart. That is the normal way.

Also be sure and promptly get the information that Monsignor Carol is supposed to send personally to me.

Since don Franco had copies of Sister Elena's letters to His Excellency on that score, and since he well knew the course of that practice from Monsignor Carol's Secretariat, he was able to make some pertinent corrections.

Your Excellency:

I am grateful for Your letter of September 28th. I had it with me when I called on Monsignor Carol. Herewith enclosed you will find the Secretary's reply. For Monsignor Carol the case is now closed: the whole matter is left in your hands. I know that Sister Elena Aiello, the Mother General, had on hand other qualified teachers, who, though not Religious, are none-the-less members of the Institute. If I showed a personal interest in conversation with Your Excellency on this matter, it never occurred to me to divulge, either by writing or by word of mouth, any of the confidential information, not even my recent appeal to you. It is not possible for me to state by letter all that I could say about the past. If Your Excellency so desire, I shall see you personally at the first opportunity. But this much I can now say: not all the Nuns have a Pontifical Assistant, who, by mandate of the Sacred Congregation, reserves everything to himself. The Sister Minims do have such a one in the person of Very Reverend Father Bonaventura da Pavullo . . .

Mother General, too, wrote as follows to His Excellency on October 9, 1956.

Your Excellency:

I herewith enclose two copies of the certificates as per your request. Miss Franca Turano—a member of our Community—is to go to Carolei and Miss Flora Alcise to S. Fili. The two additional copies concern Sister Crocifissa Vetere and Sister Rita Osso. They were mailed to Your Excellency on June 1, 1956, and to the National Federation for the Mezzogiorno d'Italia as well. I am also enclosing four copies of certificates for your Chancery Archives and a copy of State approval on November 23, 1939, for Orphanages of San Francesco di Paola at S. Fili, and of S. Luigi Gonzaga at Carolei on December 2, 1938. At present 50 children are enrolled at S. Fili and 55 at Carolei. May I hope that Your Excellency will graciously permit both Orphanages to function, as soon as possible, because people are patiently waiting.

Begging your Episcopal blessing, I am . . .

This transaction also misfired. On the other hand the Nuns were received most warmly at Pentone in the Catanzaro Diocese. Here is a letter written by the Pastor to Mother General on February 11, 1952.

Very Reverend Mother:

Your Sisters' arrival at Pentone has truly been an unforgettable event for all our people. The public manifestation of joy and of benevolence towards your Sisters has been so impulsive and enthusiastic that it is the best proof of the religious faith of our people of whom I am the unworthy Pastor. These Sisters, whom you are entrusting to my spiritual care, shall form the dearest and choicest portion of my sheepfold and therefore they shall be defended and protected with the greatest care and attention.

May our sweet Lady of Termine bless their work so that they may yield abundant fruit for the benefit of children and of our people. We feel confident that the presence of your good Sisters will serve to bring about a fast improvement in the spiritual life of our Parish for God's glory and for the salvation of souls. Thanking you for your great kindness as well as for your cherished gift and joining you in prayer, with cordial greetings and with profound gratitude, I am

Sincerely your in Christ,
FATHER VIRGILIO TARANTINO
Archpriest

On July 31, 1955, he dispatched to Mother General an accurate report dealing with the Sisters' efficient labors in the threefold field: Orphanage for little girls: Catholic Action Apostolate and Teaching of Christian Doctrine in the Parish.

The purchase of the house in Rome, which had been personally contracted by Mother General in 1957, had been preceded by a long series of efforts since 1948. Through the good offices of don Franco and some other friends, she tried first at Via di Porta Latina, then at Viale Cortina d'Ampezzo, close to Via Gallia (adjacent to the Parish) and finally at Acilia where the property consisted of a small house and about 3 acres of land. On January 22, 1951, Mother General wrote to don Franco as follows:

Very Reverend Father:

I hasten to reply to your last letter to advise you that just yesterday Miss Maria Di Marco informed me that Mrs. B., wants twenty million lire—and a few of them at the signing of the contract—for her property in the neighborhood of Via Gallia. I was really shocked because in her last letter she had assured me that fourteen million lire was all she wanted. She was to receive two million at the signing of the property deed and the remaining sum after ten years. You may get a more precise information by directly consulting Mrs. B. In case that Miss Maria's report is right, then we will have to look for some other place. I am reliably informed that the lodging houses that were used during the Holy Year, may be purchased by paying a certain sum within the period of a few years. You may also get in touch with Honorable Foderaro about that Fascio house. The enclosed blank sheets should come in handy in case you have to make a petition. In this letter you will find all the information you requested concerning our Congregation: i.e., a list with the total number of Sisters: a list of houses already established and of those we are about to open; also detailed information about the various activities of our Institute, which may be serviceable to you. It may be advisable to see the lawyer, whose address I am herewith enclosing, as he may know of some unpretentious villa that could be rented on a monthly basis.

May our Lord bless our desires. Our cordial greetings to Monsignor Sposetti and to you from Mother Vicar and myself."

The trouble was that there was no money on hand, neither was there any desire—quite praiseworthy of course—to plunge into heavy indebtedness. At last Sister Elena was able to get the money. Miss Manes had built a Home for the Aged at S. Fili, and had set aside ten million lire for the upkeep of that Institute. Now having assumed the obligation and the cost for the support of its residents, Mother General obtained the benefactor's consent to utilize the above mentioned sum for the purchase of a house in Rome.

About the middle of November 1957, she still toyed with the hope of buying the Acilia property, though an additional sum of ten million lire was needed for payment in full. On November 13, 1957, Sister Elena wrote to don Franco as follows:

> On the fifth of this month I travelled to San Lucido for the inauguration of the Home for the Aged. It was a very lovely function, thank God. The Very Reverend Father Bonaventura, who had come here on the seventh of this month, was able to call the Bishop's attention to the situation of the ex-Nuns, M., L., and M., and to give him a report of which you shall receive a copy. He would like you to suggest a way to get a ten million lire loan for the purchase of the Acilia property. Father Assistant has consented to go to Rome when the Acilia property is transferred. I would have been on my way without further delay but for the fact that Our Lord desires that I should suffer. Just now I am afflicted with ear trouble and therefore I am not in a position to travel. Should I feel some improvement, I would be leaving about November 21st or 22nd. I have so advised Mrs. Campanari.
>
> May I assure you that I am remembering all your intentions in my prayers. With best wishes from Mother Vicar and myself, I am
>
> Very devotedly yours,
>
> P.S. Father Provincial is presently in Rome. Please try your best to have him take a look at the Acilia property.

Sister Elena arrived in Rome on November 21, and was the guest of the Sisters of Santa Brigida on Via della Isole. She was accompanied by Sister Imelda and Sister M. Francesca and was ill as usual. Being unable to get the desired loan, she discarded the Acilia property and she purchased instead a house on Via dei Baldassini which, besides having three stories, is isolated and fenced in, though restricted by narrow grounds. She did so because she was in a position to offer the ten million lire on hand and also because she was willing to assume the obligation to liquidate a previous mortgage.

CHAPTER TWELVE

Rome Sides with Sister Aiello

"It is of the utmost importance for the history of our Institute—so it is written in the report of the First General Chapter—to make mention of the ecclesiastical approbation of our Congregation, through the canonical and juridical recognition from Church and State."

WE HAVE ALREADY SEEN how Archbishop Nogara had a mind to give Sister Elena's Institute a juridical recognition as a Congregation canonically established and, with Diocesan right, at least. That is the first step to obtain, later on, the recognition of pontifical right from the Holy See. This is the seal of ecclesiastical authority—a mark of authenticity that confers prestige, strength and vitality to a young Congregation. Being of one mind with the late Archbishop, Sister Elena, earnestly and fervently, requested Monsignor Aniello Calcara, the newly elected Archbishop, as soon as he had taken possession of the Archidiocese in October 1940, and showed some genuine interest in it, to graciously grant canonical recognition to the Institute. In the meantime don Franco also was trying his very best. When he got to Rome in 1941, he had the opportunity to be received by His Eminence Cardinal Cremonesi, to whom he warmly recommended the Institute and pleaded for its recognition by the Sacred Congregation. "Just bring me all the necessary documents" His Eminence graciously replied.

Very much elated by that wonderful news, don Franco informed Sister Elena, as soon as she returned to Cosenza. Somewhat embarrassed, Mother General replied: "Our Archbishop has already expressed his intention to take those documents personally to the Sacred Congregation." As usual, don Franco no longer insisted. "Just as you wish Mother—he said—the important thing is that we succeed." Thus 3 years passed by. From time to time—always quite discreetly—Mother reminded His Excellency to urge Rome about that application for the desired approbation. She was rightly worried, because in the event of the Foundress' death, in default of juridical recognition, which is always preceeded by Ecclesiastical approval, the Institute's property might have been amenable to serious dispersal, to heavy taxation and to the Ordinary's disposal. On the other hand, the war, with its devastations and with all kinds of hardships, seemed to be reason enough for that long delay. But, as soon as normal communications were resumed, i.e., from 1945 on, Sister Elena appealed to don Franco because that delay was worrying her. This time a touch of uncertainty was noticeable when she said: "Please see if you can get some news about our approbation from the Sacred Congregation." Here it is worthwhile to mention that, even when a Bishop approves a new Community having a Mother House in his Diocese, he still needs the final approbation from the Sacred Congregation of the Religious.

In our case, if the Archbishop wanted to establish Sister Elena's Institute as a Congregation of a Diocesan right, final approval had to come from Rome first. On that condition alone would the State grant juridical recognition. Having had the good fortune to get acquainted with Cardinal Lavitrano, who, at the time was Prefect of the Sacred Congregation of the Religious, don Franco pleaded with him to take an interest in the application dealing with the Sister Minims' Institute. For several years had passed since His Excellency the Archbishop had transmitted all the necessary documents to that Sacred Congregation. His Eminence graciously promised to do so.

A couple of months later, don Franco, on meeting His Eminence, reminded him about that matter of the Sister Minims' Institute. Cardinal Lavitrano felt surprised and displeased that the Sacred Congregation had taken no action in that matter.

"Please"—said he— "call on Monsignor Sposetti and tell him I am sending you."

That's how don Franco got to know Monsignor Sposetti by whom he was cordially greeted. "As you see I have your petition on my desk as well as a memo from His Eminence Cardinal Levitrano. But there is no document whatever in this Congregation. We have searched the Archives and have lost time in vain.

"Father, instead of acting surprised, please sit down and make a listing of all the documents that are needed." So he dictated eleven points, after which he said: "Please, write to Mother and tell her to prepare these documents and to have them sent to me through that Chancery Office—if she deems it convenient to do so." As a matter of fact, after repeated requests the Chancery forwarded the greater part of the documents, but withheld two or three of them for some unknown reason. This time the Sacred Congregation made an official request and so it was possible to move forward. The letters alone that were exchanged between Rome, where don Franco was teaching, and Cosenza, during the course of one year, would make, by themselves alone, quite an interesting documentary evidence.

Here is the text of the Decree forwarded directly to Mother General by the Sacred Congregation of the Religious.

Decree N. 207-46 C139

The Mother Superior together with the General Council of the Tertiary Sister Minims of the Passion of O.L.J.C. of the Cosenza Diocese has stated to the Congregation of the Religious that her Institute having sufficiently developed and having expanded to several Dioceses, is zealously laboring for the benefit of christian society. Besides the general object to attain the Sisters' sanctification by the perfect observance of Community life and of the simple vows of obedience, chastity and poverty, in compliance with the Sacred Rules and Constitutions, the Institute has the special purpose of assembling little girls, who are orphaned and abandoned, in suitable homes, where they receive christian education and learn housekeeping until such a time as they are able to earn an honest livelihood. Since the greater sanctification of the Sisters, as well as the development and the functioning of the activities under their direction, would be considerably developed by the Holy See's gracious approbation of said Institute, the petitioner has repeatedly requested it and has exhibited special Constitutions as well as credentials from some of the Bishops who are fevorably disposed to it.

The Sacred Congregation of the Religious, after due consideration of everything and particularly of the Ordinaries' consent in the above mentioned Diocese and of the favorable vote by the Committee of the Very Reverend Consultors, hereby raises the Institute of the Sister Minims of the Passion of O.L.J.C. to a Congregation of Pontifical Right according to the procedure of the Sacred Congregation and of the Constitutions which are clarified by the Sacred Congregation. A copy of said Constitutions is kept in the Archives of the Sacred Congregation, ever firm remaining the rights of the local Ordinaries, notwithstanding anything to the contrary.

Given at Rome, by the Secretariat of the Sacred Congregation. January 2, 1948.

LUIGI CARDINALE LAVITRANO—*Prefect*
F. L. E. PASETTO—*Secretary*

Sister Elena was bed-ridden when she received the joyful news and she showed the document to His Excellency on one of his occasional visits. Oh! "What wonderful news we have received!" "You are certainly stupid!" was his reply. "Without a previous canonical recognition by the Diocese, that piece of paper has no value whatsoever."

However, the account in the above mentioned report reads as follows: "All were extremely happy on hearing the unexpected news of the Pontifical approbation. Even our Archbishop himself showed his great satisfaction by the following letter."

Cosenza, February 21, 1948

To the Very Reverend Sister Elena Aiello,
Superior General of the Tertiary Minims of the Passion of O.L.J.C.

Cosenza.

The Sacred Congregation of the Religious, by a letter dated February 17, 1948, N. 207-46, has forwarded to me the Decree of Approbation of the Constitutions and of the

Congregations of the Tertiary Minims of the Passion. The date of this Decree is January 2, 1948, N. 207-46 C139. Hence, we have every reason to thank God with all our heart for this concession to my repeated requests. From the very first time I took hold of the government of the Archdiocese, I wanted to achieve this goal, because I foresaw the future possibility for good that could be accomplished by the Congregation of the Tertiary Minims of the Passion. Therefore, I sought invariably to improve their house discipline by giving them zealous Directors and also by consistently promoting the Sisters' complete formation, both religious and cultural.

In order to obtain this approbation it was indispensable for the Institute to spread its activities abroad. Hence, I encouraged the Sisters to open a few houses in the Diocese which was done with praiseworthy zeal by the two Foundresses, Sister Elena Aiello and Sister Gigia Mazza. This approbation by the Holy See comes as a deserved reward to their perseverance in a work that was not lacking in difficulties during twenty years of constant and devoted labors. For all these reasons it is my desire that I should make the presentation of the Decree quite soon, with a solemn function, at which all of the Sisters from the various houses are to be present. That function shall be concluded with a "Te Deum" in thanksgiving to God Who has been pleased to favor me, the Congregation of the Tertiary Minims of the Passion, and particularly Mother General, Mother Vicar and all the Sisters with such outstanding blessing.

As an omen of many more heavenly graces I give Mother General, Mother Vicar and all the Sisters, my special fatherly blessing."

MONSIGNOR ANIELLO CALCARA
Archbishop of Cosenza.

Thereafter the Institute obtained juridical recognition by the Presidential Decree of July 8, 1949, which was duly published in the "Gazzetta Ufficiale," 189, on August 30, 1949.

At first it looked as if the "proclamation" made so solemnly by the Archbishop in the presence of Authorities, and of many benefactors, would mark the happy conclusion of past misunderstandings, or at least give way to some hope for a long truce and for a gradual elimination of future disagreements. Instead that recognition by the Holy See seemed to stir up a feeling of retaliation as if nothing had been changed, and nothing had been

granted by Rome. Even the Summer Camps which had been introduced by Sister Elena in 1946 and had rapidly attained great success, became a source of fresh annoyance and humiliation to her in 1948. For these reasons the Sacred Congregation of the Religious decided, on the basis of accurate information from Monsignor Sposetti, from Mother General and from don Franco, to appoint a Pontifical Assistant to the Congregation of the Sister Minims. The Very Reverend Giuseppe Manzo, S.J., was chosen for that office. Under date of November 7, 1949, that Sacred Congregation named and appointed him for special reasons as Religious Assistant to that Institute for as long as the Holy See should decide.

The primary duty of a Very Reverend Assistant is to regulate the economic conditions of the Institute, according to the Sacred Cannons and Constitutions, to assist, by advice and vigilance, the Superior General and her counsellors in matters of great importance and to report each year on the Institute's status to that Sacred Congregation.

The "special reasons" referred to, a while ago, shall be better understood in the course of these remarks. The Pontifical Assistant was the official spokesman of the Sacred Congregation of the Religious. Thereafter the Institute enjoyed the privilege of presenting directly to Rome all problems arising on the spot; all the obstacles hindering its progress, as we have already seen concerning the establishment of some houses. The immediate and most important benefit resulting from the appointment of a Pontifical Assistant, was that of doing away with the Directors designated by the Archbishop, who had previously stated: "Foreseeing the future possibility for good to be accomplished by the Congregation of the Tertiary Minims of the Passion, I invariably sought to improve their house discipline by appointing zealous Directors. . ."

At the very beginning of 1941 His Excellency had assigned to that post Father Vincenzo Donnarumma, Superior of the Father Minims at Cosenza. On December 28, 1944, he was succeded by Father Francesco Sarago, who remained at Cosenza until 1947. Thereafter, Father Donnarumma was reappointed until the assignment of a Pontifical Assistant.

The conduct of Father Sarago, an exemplary religious for piety and doctrine, was especially profitable to the Institute, for he was a staunch protector in case of obstacles, and an expert and sure guide during trials that beset the life of every Community. By the enlightened direction of Sister, the Institute was rapidly marching ahead, getting ever stronger and expanding under the visible protection of Divine Providence. It only prayed for strength to overcome obstacles along the way. When that happened, Father Sarago would promptly come to its defense, within the limits of his position, but without regard to persons and without making unnecessary concessions.

On the other hand Father Donnarumma allowed himself, at times, to be frightened and, perhaps, because of a weak character and a penchant for existing conditions, he played the part of Don Abbondio to the detriment of justice. Especially during the two years of 1947-1949 he went so far as to become a spokesman for insinuations that tended to destroy the Institute by undermining the authority of Mother General. For example, he suggested the assignment of the Institute property to another entity and tried to bring about Sister Elena's retirement. He continued intriguing, even after the Holy See's approbation, by seeking to replace Mother General with some inexperienced young Nun.

There is nothing so disgusting as to see a stranger domineer in your own household, and disrupt discipline and harmony, especially when that very person, who is supposed to be a guardian angel of peace, becomes, though unconsciously, the very instrument of malfunction. In those circumstances, the energy, intelligence and, better still, the virtue of Sister Elena shone brightly. Even though deeply hurt, she was able to maintain discipline and the habitual harmony of the Community. Thus she overcame the "Director's" disruptive work. Furthermore, that trial clearly manifested the solid religious formation and inherent goodness of the Sisters who, ever true and loyal to their Mother General, carried on their work diligently and earnestly, while they were deeply upset by the manifold indignities heaped upon her.

At last, even that trial came to an end. The Very Reverend

Father Manzo, after speaking to Sister Elena, received a clear impression of the way of life in the Institute and therefore, he was quite enthused about it. He found in Mother General a spirit of obedience, the very opposite of the stubborness and disobedience quoted in justification of some one else's mistakes and obstinacy.

The following three letters testify to the good relations existing between Mother General and Father Manzo.

The Very Reverend Pontifical Assistant

Napoli.

I acknowledge your letter of the 14th inst, and I am grateful for all the good you are doing to our young Congregation. The report on our Institute was ready since last October, but I was prevented from giving it to Your Reverence on account of my worries over the regrettable events at San Sisto. I am herewith enclosing the legal papers concerning the donation deeds or the purchase of houses. As to Knight Commander Antonio Stiglino may I tell you that nothing has been settled because of the poor references submitted by D. M. of Montalto as well as by the Archbishop of Cosenza. For the Castrolibero house I only have a binder because we were unable to make the last payment of 300,000 lire and therefore we were not in a position to execute the property deed. Our landlords are good enough to waive the interest due on that sum. We own that house. At Bucita we are still living in the same house, because the Mazza family have not concluded as yet, the work on the inheritance partition. Thank God, the repair works on the house in Paola will be started soon. For St. Chiara's Convent I have taken the necessary steps with the Provveditore of Catanzaro so that work may be started as soon as possible. We do not own the house at Marano, although we take care of the administration. There is a suitable tract of land quite close to the house, which serves the needs of the Convent: the Sisters' monthly salary is 12,000 lire. May I assure you that the Sisters fare well indeed from every standpoint. Concerning the house at Pietrapaola, two Sisters have been instructed to be there on May 11, to tidy up that house. When that is done, our Community Sisters will take over. Each Sister will receive a monthly salary of 5,000 lire.

I think we should go slowly about opening the house at

S. Magno d'Aquino because it is unfit for a Community of Nuns. The financial report goes from October 1950 to October 1951. Please let me know if Your Reverence desire to have it up to date.

I am herewith enclosing all the reports from our branch houses. I shall continue to pray for your welfare as well as for the blessing of a very long life.

Begging your blessing, I am

Devotedly in Jesus Christ
SISTER ELENA AIELLO
Superior General

And now here are the two letters from Father Manzo:

May 5, 1952

Very Reverend Mother General:

Together with your letter, I have also received your registered and insured folder. I am satisfied with your suitable explanations. I both thank and congratulate you for the great work your Sisters are doing in your houses sheltering orphans and also for submitting the number of girls in each Orphanage.

Please pray for me. With every good wish, I bless both Mother Vicar and you with all my heart.

FATHER GIUSEPPE MANZO
Pontifical Assistant

Naples, March 8, 1952

Very Reverend Mother:

I am rather late answering your letter of the 27th of the past month because I have ever been on the move in Rome on account of my office as Apostolic Visitor. I am pleased to hear that Father Pasquale De Florio of the Redemptorists has conducted the Retreat for the Novices who were to make their Profession. I wish to thank and to congratulate them for having responded to the invitation of the Divine Spouse by their irrevocable consecration to Him. My fervent wish is that they ever remain faithful spouses of Jesus until death. I also warmly congratulate you for the new house you have opened outside the Diocese at Pentone. This is a remarkable progress for your Congregation. God be praised. I agree with you that the Sisters should first be sent to S. Mango d' Aquino and then later to Rossano. Please let me know, by the middle of next week, (not before because I will be away from Naples) if you have received the Archbishop's written permission for the opening of the house at S. Sisto, because now a few days have gone by since the 27th of the past month.

Please have courage and trust in the Lord. God's works always meet with opposition. Please pray for me. I bless you with all my heart.

FATHER GIUSEPPE MANZO
Pontifical Assistant

During that same year the Very Reverend Father Bonaventura was appointed Pontifical Assistant in place of the Very Reverend Father Manzo who, being quite old, found it difficult to travel up and down Italy and to attend to his many other duties. The pertinent document forwarded to Mother General is as follows:

Sacred Congregation of the Religious N.-721-49

The Sacred Congregation of the Religious, taking into account the special status affecting the Congregation of the Sister Minims of the Passion, whose Mother House is in the City of Cosenza, has decreed to appoint, as by this Decree it does appoint, the Very Reverend Father Bonaventura da Pavullo, Religious Assistant to that Institute with faculties connected with that office. It shall be the duty of the Religious Assistant to assist and guide the Superiors in charge of the Congregation, by timely counsel and diligent care. However, should a matter of greater importance occur, the Religious Assistant shall have no power to act: due recourse must be made to this Sacred Congregation. Given at Rome, September 30, 1932, anything to the contrary notwithstanding.

P. ARCHBISHOP LARRAONA
Secretary

It was Father Bonaventura's turn to continue in the above mentioned office. What he thought of Sister Elena and her work is quite evident from the letter he sent to the Sisters on the occasion of the death of their Foundress and Mother Superior. That letter was reported at the very beginning of this book.

The report to the first General Chapter, which though concise is quite significant, after quoting the letter concerning the approbation by the Holy See, goes on as follows:

"Thereafter a controversial view arose between the Archbishop of Cosenza and the Superior Council of the Institute on the juridical value of the above mentioned decree. On one hand the Archbishop maintained that the decree did not entitle the Congregation of the Sister Minims of the Passion to a recognition of Diocesan right. On the other hand the General Council was just as emphatic in asserting that by virtue of that Decree the Congregation being of pontifical right, was also by that very fact, of Diocesan right. The Sacred Congregation, having been requested to declare its mind on the matter, cleared away any doubt by a document dated June 8, 1956, No. 721-49 -C139 and forwarded it to His Excellency the Archbishop, who was to deliver the same to the Very Reverend Mother General.

1. The Institute of the Sister Minims of the Passion is, beyond doubt, a Religious Congregation of Diocesan right according to Canon 488 N. 3. In fact, the very granting of the Pro-Decree carries with it not only a merely civil status, but it implies as well an "Appositio manum Sanctae Sedis" that goes even beyond the limits required by Canon 492.

2. Still, the "decree of praise" is lacking.

3. In case it has not been previously done, the General Chapter should be summoned according to the Constitutions and to Canon Law. Moreover, the very presence of the Pontifical Assistant was sufficient proof that with the Pro-Decree of the Sacred Congregation, something decidedly new had taken place. Still Divine Providence permitted that incomprehension should continue in spite of all. No doubt, Sister Elena was the one who, more than anyone else, and almost exclusively, had to bear from day to day the hardest shocks. A brief spell would only take place when don Franco happened to be at Cosenza, three or four times a year, and just for a short time. Any occasion seemed to be favorable when it was a question of belittling the Institute of the Sister Minims and its Foundress. The particular method adopted was to deal with them as a "windblown foliage" denying any importance to the official recognition. As we have previously

related, that was the theory so bitterly exposed at the first reading of the Decree.

The Mother General, who had been bedridden for quite some time, felt greatly distressed on that account, but, just the same, she rose to her daughters' defense and strenuously fought back the constant, absurd, defaming campaign. On several occasions she had expressed her desire to don Franco, to journey to Rome in order to acquaint—if possible—the Holy Father with that deplorable situation. Finally she made up her mind in October 1953.

For a day or so she stayed with the Misses Di Marco on Gallia Street. Don Franco had Professor Giacomo Giangrasso call on her for an examination. The fact that her legs were swollen to an alarming degree up to her knees, gave the impression that it was a case either of a fracture or of something else that had to be located before removing it. Professor Giangrasso had her transferred to the "Salvator Mundi" clinic where all kinds of tests and X-rays could be easily made. Sister Elena stayed in that clinic from October 28 to November 9.

All the tests proved negative. The painful swelling affecting the legs was caused by the wounds on her feet. No use trying anything else. Still Elena had to be helped in order to stand on her feet. Soon after getting to the clinic, desiring to clear her young Congregation of any misjudgment, she told don Franco again that she was determined to try and make known to His Holiness a factual story of what had taken place. She had taken along the necessary documents for that very purpose. After mature consideration, and after taking counsel with a prudent and prominent person, don Franco called at the Secretariat of State, where he presented the petition of that humble Sister. The boundless faith of Sister Elena in the Holy See was indeed fully rewarded.

His Excellency Montini, now the Supreme Pontiff Paul VI, at the time pro-Secretary of State to His Holiness, called in person on this daughter of St. Francis of Paola who had come all the way from Calabria not so much to seek an unlikely cure to her illness, as to ask for the protection and defense for her Daughters, for the Institute, and for the proper execution of the

Decree by the Sacred Congregation of the Religious. His Excellency Montini stayed for over twenty minutes, paying close attention to Sister Elena who, from her bed, portrayed with her whole heart the regrettable—and almost incredible—position of the Archbishop that had lasted for so many years. It is not easy to describe the power of her words and her impulsive eloquence. Her fiery spirit seemed to sparkle in her pupils and gave the impression of reading the innermost thoughts of your soul. His Excellency Montini realized at once that Sister Elena was justified and he promised that her petition would be granted, for he would bring it to the attention of the Holy Father. Then he asked that all pertinent documents to be forwarded to him.

"Don't you have anybody here in Rome to entrust them with?" "Of course," Sister Elena replied, "we have Professor don Franco." So, don Franco, a few days later, delivered in good order, and in nine distinctive sections, all the documents in his possession, adding thereto a personal letter. (Rome, November 15, 1953). He stated therein that the very same documents had been delivered to the Sacred Congregation of the Religious by the Very Reverend Father Joseph, S.J., who had scrupulously examined, by the authority of the same Sacred Office, all the facts on the spot, particularly those concerning S. Fili and S. Sisto.

He stated further that, by request of Mother General and of Father Manzo, he had communicated with the Archbishop of Cosenza, with Monsignor Baldelli, with the Sacred Congregations of the Religious, of the Consistorial and of the Seminaries for the sole purpose of eliminating misunderstandings for the Institute's sake that was so dear to the people of Cosenza and especially to the poor. He ended by saying: "Mother Aiello has requested me to renew to Your Excellency her sentiments of profound and lasting gratitude before God, and that she hopes that, through your authoritative intervention, you will be able to relieve at long last the Religious Family of the Minims of the Passion from their distressing situation.

The gracious interest of His Excellency Montini is also shown by a letter that Sister Elena mailed to him, a copy of which was sent to the Reverend Assistant, as usual.

Here it is:

Cosenza, June 9, 1954

His Excellency Giovanni Battista Montini
Secretariat of State
Vatican City

Your Excellency:

May I acknowledge your most welcome letter of June 2nd, N. 32445, by which you graciously return our Easter greetings. I am very grateful for your pastoral and encouraging words spurring us on to trust in God and to patiently endure whatever He disposes for our sanctification in the performance of His Work.

Reverently kissing your hand etc. . . .

Notwithstanding the opposition by some people, even by Monsignor Sposetti, who didn't favor going any further, after a month or two, the Sacred Congregation of the Religious appointed Father Bonaventura as Visitor with a view to bring about peace between the Archbishop and the Institute. By a letter dated January 30, 1954, Mother General wrote as follows to don Franco. "When Father Bonaventura had an audience with the Archbishop, he found him very bitter. It is clear that Monsignor Sposetti had already acquainted him with everything . . . he repeated the same phrases, i.e., no recognition had been accorded to us: we are still subject to him: we need his permission to establish houses outside the Diocese, even for a house in Rome."

Father Bonaventura deemed it his duty to restrain don Franco's impatience and to proceed according to instructions. He did the right thing, according to dictates of his conscience, and thus the above quoted declaration by the Sacred Congregation of the Religious took place in 1956. His Excellency was compelled to serve notice of that declaration to the Mother General. The Institute of the Sister Minims, in virtue of the 1948 Pro-Decree, was far more than a simple congregation of Diocesan right. Thus the Diocese had been outwitted through the intervention of the Holy See. Just the same, His Excellency continued speaking about the approbation he was supposed to give, though at rare intervals, and in a more subdued tone.

The last time he did so—the very last indeed—because he died barely a week later—was at the very time the mortal remains of Sister Elena were being carried from Rome to the Chapel of the Mother House. As the Community was grieving for the loss of their beloved Foundress, the Archbishop, evidently annoyed, inquired how had they received permission for burial in the Chapel. Then, turning to Mother Vicar, he added: "Now that Sister Elena is dead, the Institute is subject to my authority and at the proper time I will appoint a Director."

These simple essays will give an idea to the Sisters how their Congregation sprouted as a tender shoot among thorns and how it was following the course marked by God in the Person of His Divine Son for all select souls and for all good works. That course is none other but the Royal Way of the Cross.

CHAPTER THIRTEEN

"Duce You Are Doomed, Unless . . ."

LET US TAKE one more look at Elena Aiello, and eagerly watch her active life. The story of a soul, just like the spiritual story of peoples, is something so intimate that it is difficult to describe it. The best part of that story is written by Angels in God's own book. All we do here is to supply only some clews.

Although we have proceeded with our story, there is still something else that we should like to record. Dr. Guido Palmardita was Prefect of Cosenza from August 8, 1936 to March 24, 1939, at the very time that Mother House was transferred to the new location. Vera, one of his children, who died in Rome in July 1937, was always close to Sister Elena Aiello from 1936 on, during the few months of her residence at Cosenza. This fine young lady from her very first association, was won over by the simplicity, the virtue and the work of Sister Elena. For that reason she used to praise both her virtues and the spirit of self-denial to her father. She had assimilated the Sister's anxiety and worry concerning the transfer of the Institute to more suitable quarters, and she was frequently heard to say: "Jesus desires that Sister Elena should be protected and helped for the sake of so many abandoned little girls. Sister Elena is all love, zeal and solicitude for them and she listens to God's voice. No matter what is done for her, it is never enough. . . ."

This was told to me by His Excellency Palmardita, who now resides in Rome. In Vera's diary (November 1936) we read as follows: "If it were in my power, I would give everything to the poor, especially to children for whom I grieve so very much. . . .

Today, I was with the holy Nun. Truly holy is Sister Elena, but her work is even more so. These dear little girls; oh, how much I love them! Some people have even much more than they need. O God have pity, have pity on them: take care of those little ones who never enjoyed a mother's smile. I would give all I have for them!"

The diary goes on: "After Vera passed away all of us became closer to Elena because we felt edified by her charitable heart. She was the sole solace to Vera's lonely mother. And what a solace! On two Fridays in March 1938, I personally attended the extraordinary phenomena together with the Major of the Carabineers and with Professor Santoro. I witnessed the painful wounds on the hands, on the feet, on the side, that bloody sweat, the visions, and in the end, the sudden transformation and disappearance of blood from that face now bright and radiant."

I shall now quote from the brief notes kept by His Excellency Palmardita some of the words pronounced by Sister Elena during the phenomenon.

Cosenza, March 24, 1938:

> Oh! let Mother shed her tears in the very side and Heart of Jesus! (Sister Elena was repeating aloud all she heard from Vera who resembled the Blessed Ones). The Heart of Jesus—Gemma Galgani and Vera are holding two lilies. Vera is now approaching me: she is sent by God to help me bear all this pain: otherwise I would pass away. Mary Magdalen is at the foot of the Cross, Martha and the Angels are now gathering the drops of blood.

April 15, 1938

> Do you wish to come with Me to Gethsemane? You shall have to suffer for sinners. . . . The sin of impurity makes man loathsome. . . . Blessed are the clean of heart, because they shall see God. The Angels draw near to Jesus and they stretch out their hands to remove the blood clotted on His eyes. It you wish to be perfect (now it's Vera speaking to her) you must cross the deseart before reaching the promised land. Euge, euge. Have courage! Each pain is like a flame scorching you, but some day Jesus will take you up to His Heaenly glory. Jesus says: "Father forgive them, for they

know not what they do." Look at the ears stained with blood, bruised by blows, rent by thorns. Yet, souls are stubbornly deaf to the voice of grace.

The soldiers are cursing: on the right hand side the good thief is saying: "Remember me when you shall enter your Kingdom." Jesus is now dead. Joseph, Martha, Magdalen, Nicodemus are preparing the linen cloth in which to wrap Jesus. Jesus is taken down from the Cross. Angels by the thousands are flying over the Cross and are accompanying Jesus.

Jesus is in Mary's arms: Martha is holding Him up: Magdalen is at His feet; the Angels are gathering His Blood. You must needs suffer for the sins of mankind: it is impurity that pierces the Heart of Jesus. A soldier's camp. Italy is going through a terrible time: but she will be safe because the Vicar of Christ resides there.

Oh, England is signing a contract with Italy but she is not sincere! "You shall have to suffer not only for sinners but for the civilization of Italy as well." On Holy Saturday, April 17, 1938, at 5 a.m., the Risen Savior appears to Elena saying: "Arise and fight!"

On the thirtieth day of Vera's death, Sister Elena wrote to her parents as follows:

Cosenza, July 15, 1938

I wish to thank you for that very beautiful photo which Is for us a most welcome souvenir of our unforgettable Vera. Her charming poise, her sweet and chaste smile, her truly lofty spirit shall live on and shall never be forgotten by all those who had the privilege to know and to love her. Ever a leader in all charitable activities, she was a comforting Angel to my abandoned little ones. She always had a kind and cheerful word for them and ever counselled them to love life and to be grateful for it. . . . It doesn't seem possible that she is no longer with us. . . . We seem to see her from time to time, we converse with her, we speak to her of our needs and to her we direct our frequent and fervent prayer. On the thirtieth day of her death we had a Mass offered up for her in our Chapel: our little ones set on the catafalque the most beautiful flowers of our garden, those flowers she loved so well.

The kindergarten inside the Mother House was built by His Excellency Palmardita, at his own expense, and was dedicated to Vera.

In one of her letters, Mother General mentions how prosperous her Institute was at the time of Archbishop Nogara and Prefect Palma.:dita.

Cosenza, June 28, 1947

Your Excellency:

On returning from Rome I deem it my duty to thank you for your kindness to me. We have been speaking so much about you to our Community, that they are anxiously waiting for your visit here at Cosenza. Let us hope you will do so, as soon as possible, and that your presence will be an omen of such good for our Institute, as in former times.

With sentiments of esteeem to Mrs. Palmarita, to the charming young ladies and to you. . . .

His Excellency Palmardita spoke about Sister Elena to Mussolini, who was greatly interested, even to the point of making a considerable contribution to the Cosenza House. This precedent explains why the Duce was so perturbed on receiving Sister Elena's letter just before the beginning of the Second World War. The "Giornale d'Italia" published that letter on March 19, 1956. Don Franco read it at Rome on May 2nd, the time when Sister Elena came there to attend the Canonization of Gemma Galgani. He himself delivered it to the Duce's sister, that kind, unpretentious, lovable Lady Edvige.

Cosenza, April 23, 1940

To the Head of the Government
Benito Mussolini

Duce:

I come to you in God's Name to tell you what God has revealed to me and what He wants from you. I was hesitating to write, but yesterday, April 22, the Lord appeared to me again, and bid me to tell you what follows:

The world is going to ruin because of its many sins, particularly the sins of impurity, which have presently exceeded the very limits before the Justice of My Heavenly Father.

Therefore, you shall suffer and shall become an atoning victim for the world, especially for Italy where My Vicar on earth resides. My Kingdom is a Kingdom of peace: whereas the whole world is entangled in War. The Nations' Rulers are bent on acquiring new possessions: Poor fools! They don't know that, when there is no God, there is no victory either. Their hearts are filled with wickedness. All they do is to outrage, ridicule and despise Me. They are like devils sowing dissension, subverting people and seeking to drive into the sinful scourge of war even Italy, when God is pleased with many souls, and where My Vicar on earth, the Pastor Angelicus, resides. France, so dear to My Heart, shall soon fall to ruin on account of her many sins, and shall be overthrown and ravaged like the ungrateful Jerusalem. I sent Benito Mussolini to preserve Italy from the precipice because of My Vicar on earth: otherwise, by now, she would be worse off than Russia.

I have always shielded him from many dangers. He must now keep Italy out of war, because Italy is a civilized country and it is the dwelling place of My Vicar on earth. If he is willing to do this, he shall receive many favors and I shall make all Nations respect him. But since he has made up his mind to go to war, tell him that, if he doesn't prevent it, he will be punished by My Divine Justice.

It is the Lord Who has told me all this. Please, Duce, don't think for a moment that I am interested in politics. I am just an ordinary Nun looking after the welfare of abandoned little girls, and I am earnestly praying for your safety as well as the safety of our Country.

Respectfully,
SISTER ELENA AIELLO

That letter was delivered on May 6, 1940, to Donna Edvige, the Duce's sister, who handed it to Mussolini a day or so later. We find an allusion thereto in the following letter to Donna Edvige.

Montalto, Uffugo, May 15, 1943

My dear Donna Edvige:

You may have thought that, on account of my long silence, I may have forgotten you, whereas I remember you every day in my prayers. I am following the painful events now taking place in our beautiful Italy. We have left Cosenza on account of the bombardments. The enemy's barbarity has vented all its hatred by bombing the City of Cosenza thus bringing desolation and death to the population. I was bedridden because of my illness: three bombs fell close to our Institute, but the Lord, in His infinite goodness and mercy, has protected us. We have taken refuge at Montalto Uffugo, my native town, in order to protect the little girls from the danger of new raids.

Naturally, we are far from comfortable, but we are offering up all to God for the preservation of Italy. The purpose of this letter is that I wish to make another appeal to you, just as I did in the month of May 1940, when I was introduced to you in Rome by Baroness Ruggi for the purpose of giving you in writing whatever God had revealed to me concerning the Duce.

If you recall, on May 6, 1940, we were saying that the Duce had made up his mind to go to war, whereas, the Lord had warned him in my letter to keep Italy out of war, otherwise His Divine Justice would strike him. "I have always rescued him—said Jesus—from many a danger: now it is up to him to save Italy from the scourge of war because Italy is the dwelling place of My Vicar on earth. If he complies with My request, I will bestow great blessings on him and I shall cause all Nations to respect him, but, since he is determined to go to war, I want him to know that, if he persists, he will be severely punished by My Justice."

Ah! Had the Duce only listened to Jesus' words, Italy wouldn't be in such a terrible plight now. . . . I know that the Duce must feel quite dejected on seeing Italy, once a flourishing garden, now a barren field filled with diseases and deaths. But, why persist in this terribly cruel war, when Jesus has stated that no one is going to achieve true victory?

Therefore, my dear Donna Edvige, please tell the Duce, in my name, that this is God's last warning to him. He is still in time to save himbelf by leaving all things in the hands of the Holy Father. Should he be unwilling to do so —said the Lord—Divine Justice shall quickly reach him. The other Rulers also, who play deaf to the counsel and directives of My Vicar, shall be overtaken and punished by My Justice.

Do you recall that, on July 7th of last year, you asked me what was in store for the Duce Didn't I reply that, if he didn't listen to the Pope, he would wind up worse than Napoleon? Now I am going to repeat the very same words, "If the Duce is unwilling to rescue Italy and ignore the Holy

Father, he will have a speedy downfall." Even Bruno is begging his father from the other world to save both Italy and himself. Quite often Our Lord says that Italy will be protected on account of the Pope, who is the atoning victim for this disaster. Therefore, the only way to achieve true peace in the world, is the one that the Holy Father shall indicate.

My dear Donna Edvige, please, remember that whatever Our Lord revealed to me has been perfectly fulfilled. Who has been the cause of all this ruin to Italy? Isn't it the Duce's fault? Didn't he refuse to listen to the warnings of Our Lord Jesus Christ? Even now, he could somehow counteract the evil done provided he be willing to do what God wants of him. As for me I shall continue to pray for that intention.

A reminder of this correspondence with Lady Edvige is evident in the following letter which needs no comment.

To the Very Reverend Sister Elena Aiello
Superior of the Institute S. Teresa del B. Gesu
Cosenza
Rome, Holy Year 1950

Very Reverend Mother:

Seven years ago I had the honor and pleasure to be received by you in the Convent of the Suore di Malta, Via Iberia, Rome. Since that day I never forgot that pleasant hour I passed in your company. I begged of you a special favor which I received. How could I have ever forgotten meeting a Saint? I find no words to tell you, my Very Reverend Mother, how often, in my distress as Mother and Sister, I have thought of you and of those prophetic words you wrote to me at the very beginning of the war. In April 1945, I lost my brother, my twenty-one year old son Joseph and the husband of my eldest daughter. All of them were murdered on the same day in Northern Italy.

My Very Reverend Mother, I don't know how I could have survived such a dreadful ordeal. God alone knows, since it is He Who is keeping me alive. As if all that were not enough, I am constantly besieged by trials and worries.

Just now my daughter Maria Teresa, mother of two children, besides being in poor health, is in poor financial circumstances. If her husband succeeds in winning a lawsuit, they could get along fairly well, but, unless God and His

Saints come to his aid, I doubt that justice will be done. I also have my only son Paul, who, in mid-October will have to undergo his two final examinations previous to graduation. Since he was unable to attend the regular course during the past six years, on account of all his sufferings during and after the war, he finds it rather hard now to keep up with his studies.

Very Reverend Mother, under these trying circumstances affecting my poor children, so badly in need of help, I beg of you, with joined hands, to pray that God's blessing may descend upon them. Fully confident you will grant my request, embracing you in Christ and with my best wishes to your Sister and to you I am

Affectionately yours,
EDVIGE MANCINI MUSSOLINI

During wartime, the little girls at the Mother House were always given good bread through the kindness of the Leonetti Family. Naturally their transfer to Montalto Uffugo was far from pleasant, and the losses caused by the bombardments were very heavy. A good number of the 16 machines for sewing and knitting were destroyed, others were damaged. Desks, tables, blackboards, chairs . . . everything had to be replaced.

After listing to the various losses to the Treasury Department, the statement continues.: "This is one of the oldest establishments for technical instruction in the Province of Cosenza, having won prizes at several exhibitions. At present it is not in a condition to function because Sister Elena, the undersigned, states further that the little abandoned girls, daughters of veterans and of the unemployed are trained in our establishment with free but temporary courses, organized by the Provincial Syndicate for such institutions." Then she also mentioned other activities such as grammar schools, cafeterias for school children, orphanages and other charitable works.

The period of reconstruction was slow, but benefactors distinguished themselves by their generous donations. Sure enough the change in Government didn't make things any easier, because the attitude of the Church Authorities found a conterpart in the very Prefecture. Moreover, on August 28, 1943, Sister Elena, while crossing the Corso Mazzini at Cosenza in a bus, was suddenly knocked to the floor. She had barely saved the little girl close to her. As a result, she sustained several fractures which forced her to spend most of the day either in bed or on an easy chair. She could hardly stand on her feet, and any movement caused her a great deal of pain. Nevertheless, either from her cell or from the loggia of the nearby hall, she was ever watching over the Institute that Divine Providence had entrusted to her.

Don Franco well remembers the activities of Mother General from that cell during the summer months. Yet, sometimes, she could only take a piece of ice in her mouth, and, at long intervals, because she could not retain any food. Every morning, as soon as she had straightened out her room, she would wait for the Priest, who, after saying Mass in the Chapel, would come up and give her Holy Communion. For she was no longer able to get down to the Chapel, except on rare occasions, and with great effort. Only on some feast days permission would be granted to have Mass said on a portable altar, either in her cell or in an adjoining room that was decorated as a Chapel. Thereafter, she would give the daily assignments to the Sisters.

The Novices too would come up with one of the Superiors after Meditation and Holy Mass in order to receive her blessing and some appropriate advice. Then, as soon as the mail arrived, Mother would promptly attend to her correspondence either by outlining a reply or by dictating the letter to the Sister in charge. Besides the business of the Institute, besides the problems of the other houses, she had to answer letters from benefactors and from some unknown people from every section of Italy and also of North America. They all turned to her in their trials and tribulations, seeking advice and begging prayers for themselves and for their dear ones.

Sister Elena's earnest gratitude to the benefactors of her Institute is quite evident by the warm way she shared their grief at a time of mourning. Her letters on such occasions are so beautiful that one seems to detect therein the warm charity of the great soul that inspired them. I shall, for example, quote a letter she sent to don Franco shortly after his mother's death.

Cosenza
November 9, 1954

Very Reverend Professor:

I am rather late acknowledging your letter because I had heard from Miss Anna that you had gone to Salerno. May I say that both we and our dear ones had been worrying a great deal over your journey to Salerno. Miss Anna, don Peppino, and Gigino, who is still disconsolate over grandmother's passing, came here last Sunday. Of course, though quite ill, her presence was always a great source of consolation during all family events. As for us, we who knew only too well the beauty of her soul, so good and kind, and assisted her up to the very last moment of her life, this separation has been even more painful. On the other hand that beautiful soul so rich in merits and truly exemplary for her christian resignation during her long illness is now already enjoying God's presence. From heaven she will be watching over and protecting you, and by her earnest intercession she shall continue to guide you in the way of goodness of which she has left you such a wonderful example.

The contemplation of her glory and eternal happiness should relieve your sorrow and, sanctify your love for her and help you share her happiness. For, from the other world, she can love you and protect you far better than when she was on earth. Without fail we shall daily remember her in our prayers and we earnestly hope that, through her protection over you and our Institute, she will be an instrument of a new era of peace and prosperity.

With kindest regards from Mother Vicar and from myself, kissing your hand etc. . . ."

Although bedridden, she was always available to all those who came to see her about the more important business of the Institute. Whenever don Franco happened to be in Cosenza, every morning, after saying Mass in the Chapel, he would go upstairs and exchange a few words with Mother. Afterwards the Superiors of different houses would come up and they would be greeted with motherly predilection and with a loving smile so expressive of her joy and satisfaction. Other people too, hailing from afar, would call on her to be enlightened in their trials, to seek relief in their troubles, or to hear a word of trust in God, at the time of some hopeless situation.

There are times when our thoughts are just like prayer. Then our soul seems to be bending low before God, no matter what the body's posture might be. That was the habitual way with Sister Elena's soul. Being in union with Jesus Crucified, she possessed the faculty to impart to others her own faith, her vigor, her calm, all of which of course, was the fruit of her filial surrender to Divine Providence.

Alas! How deserving of pity are they who are engrossed only with material things, because death shall suddenly snatch away all things. On the other hand, if you love souls, you shall find them again some day. Under these circumstances Elena, like a good mother, never minded the time: she aimed only at preparing people to accept suffering and misfortune in a spirit of resignation, because it is the duty of the faithful to be lovingly submissive to the Will of God. She knew how to be silent when listening to the story of a soul in distress and she knew also when it was time for her to speak. Oh, how truly compassionate she was! She never tried to blot out a sorrow by merely ignoring it, but she rather sought to exalt it through faith and hope. Knowing that faith still abides in the hearts of the faithful, she managed to console them and to stir up hope in the hearts of those who approached her at the time of despair. Most of the time people hurried to Sister Elena when misfortune was about to strike. Then not only would she pray, but she would also pledge the prayers of the little ones. Thus she kindled the flame of hope and resignation in anguished souls.

About one year or so before 1950, having returned to Cosenza, as usual for the Christmas holydays, don Franco found his family exceedingly alarmed. In fact his 73 year old mother had been stricken with an internal hemorrhage which portended a very serious condition. In fact, according to the diagnosis, there was no further hope for her. The medical report had been confirmed by the histological examination. Don Franco instead of entering his house, went straight to the Mother General.

He found her at her usual post of work and recollection, i.e., in bed with her little white mantle on her shoulders as usual, and with a rosary in her hands. "Mother—said he—I pleaded with you so much for mother's health." Then he briefly informed her about the case. Sister Elena seemed to enter into deeper recollection. She remained deep in thought and silent for a little while. Then with the greatest calm: "Don Ci' " she said, "there is nothing to worry about. Take her to Rome: there she will receive radium treatments and everything will be well with her." Don Farnco didn't hesitate a moment. On returning home, he assured the members of his family of his complete confidence. So they enjoyed the Chirstmas holyday as usual, and the following morning on December 26, they left for Rome. There Professor Cattaneo, after verifying the diagnosis started treating the patient in the very manner indicated by Sister Elena. After the second treatment, every trace of the illness completely disappeared. Beaming with joy, the doctor said: "If any specialist came to visit your mother, he would say that our diagnosis was a mistake."

This same don Franco, on his return to Cosenza in July 1950, being very much worried on account of a personal matter, went directly to Mother and disclosed everything to her. This concerned a charge that, though untrue, was quite serious. She remained silent for a little while, as usual, then she said. "Every cloud has its silver lining." You shall return to Rome in October and, within fifteen days, you will receive your appointment to teach. Then she added smilingly, "Why, you don't even know how to defend yourself.". Everything came true, just as Sister Elena had foretold, because don Franco received his appointment exactly fifteen days after his return to Rome.

This is the reason why benefactors considered themselves debtors to the holy Nun: for they received far more than what they could do for her and her Institute. Many families indeed firmly believed that Sister Elena, by her prayers and sufferings, acted as a lightning rod for their safety, so great was their confidence in her.

As a rule perfect silence was observed during the early afternoon hours which were reserved for meditation and prayer. Thereafter the work of correspondence and of all other routine tasks was resumed till evening. Often she would have Mother Vicar with her during the evening prayers.

Sister Elena confided to don Franco that sometimes, during

the long quiet hours of the night, she would either make plans, make decisions or solve problems, and then submit them to the judgment of competent persons. Frequently, she would speak about night visits and about her conversation with some of the faithful departed who, during their lifetime, had had some kind of association with her and with her Institute. Thus she saw in her cell the mother of don Franco seated on the armchair, close to her bed, and conversing with her for nearly twenty minutes. Again on an early morning the entire Mother House was shaken by a loud explosion that blasted open the door to Sister Elena's cell. Sister told all those who had rushed upstairs that the late Father P. Donnarumma had just come in to thank her for all the fervent prayers the Community had offered to God for the repose of his soul.

Let us now take a look at the plan of the Mother House. On the ground floor there is the room of Mother Vicar, from which she supervises all the House activities, i.e., the workroom, the kitchen, the garden, plus the regular routine affecting all the household duties. The great advantage of obedience consists in this, that every individual does his work which, in turn, is completed by the rest of the Community. Worry and anxiety stop right there; for these are taken care of from on High. During the day everybody is busy at work, and all the religious exercises in the Chapel, as well as recreation and meals, are always held in common.

At last the little ones could now enjoy air, light and sun so much needed for their healthy growth. This is evident by glancing from the open courtyard at the green hills and mountains of the Sila towering over it to the East, while to the West flows the Crati gently rustling along the garden border.

Watching over all from her cell—from that bed which has been her workbench, as it were for the past two years—Mother General sees to it that her little girls be perfectly at ease, just as other girls would feel in their own homes. It goes without saying that the religious formation takes first place. One of the outstanding features of Archbishop Nogara's pastoral activity was the impulse he gave to the formation of our people. Many persons recall the contests he initiated and the prizes he awarded for that purpose. The diplomas and relative prizes of gold, silver and bronze medals are kept in Sister Elena's Institute. This kind of activity was carried on without interruption as the following letter shows.

The Young Ladies, Catholic Action for Italy
Consenza
September 27, 1955

Very Reverend Mother General

Sister Elena Aiello:

During the few years I have been in Calabria, as regional director of the Young Ladies' Catholic Action, I am glad to give witness, without fear of exaggeration, to the great deal of good your Sisters have been accomplishing in our Diocese. I have had the opportunity to know them well, on several occasions, during my apostolic activity. What a joy to see that, besides a solid piety, they also practiced true charity in all fields, particularly where children are concerned, according to your banner motto: "Charitas." The presence of your Sisters was and is truly beneficial and providential for the welfare of souls, to the many villages that are deprived of everything. Quite often your houses serve as quarters for Catholic Action. They may be poor and small in size, but there is real warmth in them and a great deal of generosity in welcoming girls of any age and social condition. They in turn, being spiritually strengthened, are in a position to take care of their youth with great diligence and confidence.

May God grant your Houses to expand throughout the greater part of the Calabrian region. And may you, Mother, be favored from Above with that recognition you so richly deserve, and that we so much desire for your sacred Institution whose benefits we experience every day.

With kindest regards.

Franca Maltese,
Regional Delegate

The Religious training does bear fruitful results, when it sets out from, and is accompanied with, the highest motive of charity. No one could match the interest Sister Elena displayed for every child. Here is what she wrote on February 4, 1952, concerning an orphan boy.

Please tell Monsignor Sposetti how grateful I am for his wonderful charity to Franco. (Monsignor had tried to place that 12 year old boy in some Roman Institute) Oh how good God is, and how well does He protect the orphans! Just when Franco was about to leave for Rome, something quite unexpected happened. They say that one should not believe in dreams, but, at times, they do really come true. A lady whose son Franco, had died, had a dream about her late mother. She was told not to weep but to go to our Institute where there was another boy by the name of Franco. So the married couple came to see him, and on January 29th they took him away. They are now making arrangements with Counsellor Cribari for his legal adoption.

I am very happy both for Franco and for Anna, the orphan girl we have brought up since she was sixteen years old. We have now settled both Franco and Anna. Anna earns her own livelihood. Franco came to see me! He looks like a real gentleman."

At times, besides the ordinary duties, some extraordinary matters had to be attended to, as for example, planning either for exhibitions or for summer camps. One could truthfully say that in 1946 Sister Elena was the only one in the Archdiocese of Cosenza to resume the fine work of the summer camps, which previously had been carried out by fascism. From the very beginning Sister Elena had called on Miss Emmanuela Travo—an expert in the matter of summer camp organization. While preparations were being made for that purpose, the Mother House resembled—and it does so even now—the general quarters and central supplies of an army. If everything was carried out to perfection, that was simply due to the care, the enthusiasm and the sacrifices involved in the preparation of that work. And even then how many obstacles had to be overcome in order to insure its success!

Whenever she was to start some important project, Sister Elena would leave her room and, by sheer will-power, would make herself useful by way of imparting some pertinent instructions. That is the way she acted concerning San Sisto's House, the purchase of the house in Rome and for the best interests of the Institute. For that reason she did not hesitate to take long trips, even though she was suffering a lot. During the first year of the summer camps, i.e., in 1946, besides looking after the usual arrangements, she went to the house at Paola and she stayed there for nearly three months. Her last visit to that house was June 24, 1957. She also went several times to the big house at Montalto while the work of reconstruction was going on. In the report prepared for the First General Chapter on November 15, 1958, mention is made of several activities.

The Congregation now numbers 135 Sisters; Perpetual Vows, 47; Temporary Vows 49; Novices 8; Postulants 10; and Aspirants 20. The Sister Graduates in cutwork, sewing, embroidering, and knitting are 47. The professional workshop has greatly developed during the last few years by improving its products and by exhibiting at the fair in Cosenza for 5 consecutive years. The prize of 500,000 lire was won during the first year. Three additional fairs are conducted each year at Paola, Montalto and Pentone.... The Orphanage at the Mother House takes care of nearly 100 boys during the day. Our Sisters teach the catechism in 6 City Churches and in the countryside of Caricchio and Guarassano... The Camps from 1946 to 1954 have been held either during the day or during the night. From 1954 to 1956, they have been in operation only during the day except at Paola.

Now about the Catholic Action within the Institute. There are more than 110 girls at the Mother House: 50 of them are boarded through several organizations: all the others are kept at no charge. They remain in the Community until they are definitely settled, for that is the specific object of our Constitution. Here is some additional information concerning the other Houses. Our Congregation accounts altogether for 340 boarding girls. Of course, it might have achieved greater expansion but for the many peculiar obstacles along the way.

That's how it was by the end of 1956. Obviously God was blessing all those holy enterprises which depended solely upon Him. In fact Sister Elena trusted in Divine Providence with a childlike confidence. Hence, she offered up her prayers and had the Sisters and the orphan girls do the same in order to gain the blessing of the Almighty.

CHAPTER FOURTEEN

Jesus' Face Bleeding on a Wooden Panel

ON MARCH 25, 1967, Father Francesco Mazza forwarded to Archbishop Calcara the report he had requested, concerning the phenomenon of the blood sweat as well as of the profile of Jesus' Face that had appeared on a masonite panel in Sister Elena's cell. For a few years some square pieces of masonite had been set on the wall adjoining Sister Elena's bed to protect her somewhat from the cold and dampness caused by water running through a battery of faucets in an adjoining closet.

During the extraordinary phenomenon, and especially on Good Friday, a few drops of blood which had squirted from the patient's face, had stayed on, and had dried up on the masonite, which was level with the bed pillows. On September 29, 1955, Feast of St. Michael the Archangel, protector of the Order of the Minims, Sister Elena had fervently prayed to the Archangel invoking his help and protection. About midnight Sister Luisa Prena, the nurse, was giving her some camphor drops, when suddenly a light flashed on the left lower corner of the panel. Very much surprised at the sight, the two Sisters looking closely saw blood dripping from the dried drops on the panel. Sister laid her fingers on the masonite and, on withdrawing them, beheld them stained with blood. In the morning she noticed that the white coverlet close to the masonite was soaked with blood. That was the beginning of a phenomenon defying description. On the blood soaked cotton tufts, and on the linen that had touched the panel, several forms or designs showed through, such as, a cross, a crown or a heart. Father made sure to enclose all the pertinent pictures.

The blood continued to flow from that panel from midnight September 29 to October 13.

The same phenomenon happened again on November 1st and 21st, also on December 8, 1955. Again on January 6, March 3, April 2 and, in a more remarkable way, on May 3rd, Feast of the Holy Cross: on June 8, Feast of the Sacred Heart and, more profusely than ever, on the Feast of the Most Precious Blood on July 8, 1956. On this last date Sister Elena washed the masonite with water seven times, but the blood continued to flow during the entire day. The features of a face started to appear clearer and more distinct on the panel especially on feast days connected with the Mysteries of the Passion and Death of Our Lord.

The blood flows especially from the eyes of that picture which recalls to mind the Image of Jesus during His Passion. That picture, visible even now, is staying there for good. In November 1956, Father Bonaventura da Pavullo, the Pontifical Assistant, happened to be staying at the Mother House in order to preside at the First General Chapter. On November 23rd at 7:30 a.m., on the eve of his departure, the blood started to flow once more from that panel. Father not only soaked the handkerchief with it but he gathered also enough blood for a test, which proved to be human blood. This same phenomenon continued at intervals during the succeeding years up to Sister Elena's death.

Professor Schettini, the City's Mayor and an outstanding physician, together with other public officials came to see Sister Elena for the purpose of taking a good look at that picture on the masonite panel. Quite a few were able to notice how slowly the blood was flowing, and, in his report, Father Francesco gave even the visitors' names, and the date on which the event had taken place.

It is now interesting to quote a few remarks from an anonymous report of 1957 concerning a visit to the Superior General, Sister Elena Aiello. "Blood started to trickle down even more intensely from the panel during the first days of October 1955.

I happened to be there during those days, and so I was able to place a handkerchief at the base of the panel. When I removed it, it was soaked with blood. That phenomenon has recurred time and again, as a rule, during solemnities connected with the sufferings of Our Most Holy Redeemer and of His Mother, the Blessed Virgin Mary.

The picture of a face exuding blood, which gradually appeared on the masonite a short while after the phenomenon started, is there to stay and it is perfectly visible to all.

After a whole year had gone by I glanced at the picture that was still there. Yes, more than one year had passed from that morning of October 1st, when the white linen touching the masonite was washed with soda, yet the phenomenon started again. The photo clearly reproduces the picture which still remains unchanged. Moreover, the chemical test has clearly established that here we are looking at human blood.

Quite naturally our thoughts go back to the wonderful event *of* the tears shed by Our Lady of Syracuse. It is not for us to judge facts that, humanly speaking, cannot be explained: it is sufficient that they have been duly controlled and that they actually happened. It is natural also that we should inquire about the meaning of that phenomenon. Why this blood? Do these extraordinary events portend any significant message? I have here on hand a bit of paper that perhaps gives a clue to the right solution. Its contents are very serious indeed. They resemble a page of the Apocalypse, containing, as they do, urgent warnings, appalling forebodings and a clear intuition that takes in all nations and also the fundamental reasons for all the human events.

Here are some of the more notable excerpts: "People are offending God too much. Were I to show you all the sins that are committed on a single day, you would surely die of grief. These are grave times. The world is thoroughly upset because it is now in a worse condition than at the time of the deluge. Materialism marches on ever fomenting bloody strifes and fratricidal struggles. Clear signs portend that peace is in danger. That scourge, like the shadow of a dark cloud, is now moving across mankind: only my power, as Mother of God, is preventing the outbreak of that storm. All is hanging on a slender thread. When that thread shall snap, Divine Justice shall pounce upon the world and execute its dreadful, purging designs. All the Nations shall be punished because sins, like a muddy river, are now covering all the earth.

The powers of evil are getting ready to strike furiously in every part of the globe. Tragic events are in store for the future. For quite a while, and in many a way, I have warned the world. The Nations' Rulers do indeed understand the gravity of these dangers, but they refuse to acknowledge that it is necessary for all people to practice a truly christian life to counteract that scourge. Oh, what torture I feel in my heart, on beholding mankind so engrossed in all kinds of things and completely ignoring the most important duty of their reconciliation with God. The time is not far off now when the whole world shall be greatly disturbed. A great deal of blood of just and innocent people as well as of saintly Priests will be poured out. The Church shall suffer very much and hatred will be at its very peak.

Italy shall be humiliated and purged in her blood. She shall suffer very much indeed on account of the multitude of sins committed in this privleged Nation, the abode of the Vicar of Christ.

You cannot possibly imagine what is going to happen. A great revolution shall break out and the streets shall be stained with blood. The Pope's sufferings on this occasion may well be compared to the agony that will shorten his pilgrimage on earth. His successor shall pilot the boat during the storm. But the punishment of the wicked shall not be slow. That will be an exceedingly dreadful day. The earth shall quake so violently as to scare all mankind. And so the wicked shall perish according to the inexorably severity of Divine Justice. If possible, publish this message throughout the world, and admonish all the people to do penance and to return right away to God.

In her cell, usually so quiet, Sister Elena continues fulfilling her supernatural work of charity through the christian education of her orphan girls. There, close to her bed the panel goes on dripping blood. She doesn't talk about it, perhaps because she wouldn't know just what to say. But she knows that sin—

not suffering—is the only real evil in this world. She is sure that in the end God's Kingdom shall triumph and that's good enough for her. That blood dripping from the wooden panel, and the picture protrayed thereon, are no doubt a sign, a witness from heaven, sanctioning the life and work of Sister Elena. And, of course, it is a lesson for us all.

The few items kept in that cell that is now empty, recall to mind the image of that valiant woman, who closely followed the Passion of Our Lord for nearly 23 years during the Lenten Fridays and, especially so, on Good Friday. Thus, by prayer and suffering, she made ready for the glory of the Resurrection."

CHAPTER FIFTEEN

The Repose

WE ARE ABOUT to close our few remarks. By quickly glancing at them we realize that a great deal has been left unsaid. The reader will have to fill in some of the omissions by just a little reflection. For example, from the few letters we have quoted, he may form a good idea of the highest regard this daughter of St. Francis of Paola had for the virtues of friendship, of gratitude, or for any other commendable attribute. Many events bear out the truth of this statement. We just mention a couple of them as related by don Franco. After the successful conclusion of one of her many trials . . . don Franco en entering Mother's cell, found her in tears on her bed, "Didn't I plead with you—said he—not to pay any attention to . . . these persecutions . . ." "It's not that—Sister replied—I am weeping for the harm he is doing to his soul . . ."

On one Summer afternoon, when Mother was in her cell outlining her plans to don Franco and to another Priest about a Chapel that a gentleman wanted to donate to the Congregation, the latter abruptly and rudely butted in with some offensive remarks to her. Don Franco, completely stunned, glanced quickly at Sister Elena. Sure enough she was just as calm and collected as you and I would have been on hearing someone praising us to the sky.

The reader will forgive us for our considerable omissions in this book and also for having related events in the only way it was possible for us to do so. We do earnestly hope that, as soon as a better source of information is at hand, it will be possible to give our readers a more adequate presentation of the life and work of Sister Elena Aiello.

The thought of our heavenly home was ever present to Sister Elena's mind, for she used to talk about her death quite frequently. To don Franco—who thoroughly enjoys the nickname, "the homeless man," she said several times: "When I am about to die, you shall be the one to assist me. You shall be that very one." In 1961, besides her usual chronic diseases, she was afflicted with a persistently high fever which the physicians were unable to explain or cure. She had been suffering that way for nearly two months, when she expressed a desire to go to Rome.

Because of her condition, everybody, the physicians included, were against her taking that trip. Nevertheless, Mother had made up her mind and so, together with Mother Vicar and Sister Maria Silvana, she left Cosenza on the evening of June 7th. The following morning, June 8, she was greeted at the railroad station by Sister Imelda, Superior of the House in Rome, and by Madams Anna Romanazzi, Diomira Piccini, Marcella and Vittoria Quaranta, who had always shown the keenest interest in Sister Elena and in her work. Since the route from Termini to Via dei Baldassini was rather long, Sister had previously expressed a desire to ride in the car of Madam Romanazzi, who was overjoyed. Her arrival was a real surprise. She said to don Franco, who had hastened to welcome her: "This time I am going for good."

Neither the persistent fever nor the difficult breathing alarmed him because he knew very well that the thought of death and a life of suffering were quite normal to Sister Elena. Dr. Raffaello Liberti, a clinical expert and chief surgeon at the S. Giovanni's Hospital, had the patient transferred to the hospital in order to keep her under observation and practice the necessary tests. Sister Elena let them do as they pleased, and so, on June 12, she was moved to room No. 1 on the sixth floor of the new S. Giovanni's Hospital, in the neighborhood of the Lateran on the Ambaradam Street.

On Sunday, June 18, at 7 P.M., Sister Imelda asked her if she could start the recitation of the Rosary, because it was time for prayer. Sister Elena made a gesture with her hand to wait for a moment: then she herself started saying the Rosary and continued reciting it aloud. About 10:30 P.M., Sister Imelda, feeling worried on account of Mother's condition getting worse, telephoned to don Franco who came right away. Besides seeing the Superior who was in the patient's room, he also met in the hallway Sister M. Emma, Sister Silvana and Sister Teodolinda, who were weeping. With them too was Madam Marcella, who stayed there the whole night. Showing great energy and assuming all responsibility, Sister Imelda had the patient removed to the Roman House where Mother Vicar was waiting. As soon as she got into the ambulance, because of the oxygen inhalation and of the attentive medical care, Sister Elena opened her eyes and seemed to be herself again.

It was 11:30 P.M.

The male nurses, Sister Imelda and don Franco were inside the ambulance. Madam Marcella was seated in front. The journey from Ambaradam Street to Via dei Baldassini, during that bright night in June, seems now like a dream. With the same gentle care as before, the patient was carried to the same small room on the ground floor. Here she was able to recognize Mother Vicar: in fact, she pointed out aloud to her and asked for some water. Father Salvatore Schembri, pastor of the adjoining Church of S. Maria della Perseveranza, came in at once and saw also the district physician Dr. Mario Lucciarini who, after adjusting the flow of oxygen, prescribed some injections. Then at don Franco's request, Dr. Adele Pignatelli, the foundress of the Ladies' Medical Missionary Society, was ushered in, and she, with exemplary self-denial, stayed with Doctor Luisa Guidotti of the same association at the patient's bedside until morning. About 2 A.M., the pastor, assisted by don Franco, administered Extreme Unction, and then together they began reciting the prayers for the dying. At 5:30 A.M., don Franco said the Holy Mass in the Chapel almost opposite Mother's room. As soon as the Mas was over, Sister Elena stopped breathing and thus her long suffering came to an end. It was about 6:19 A.M.

"Your dearly beloved Mother General . . . wrote Father Bonaventura has taken her flight to heaven, at dawn, while the rays of the morning sun were lighting up the sky, during the profound silence of people and things. Both her first and favorite daughters and the chirping of the early birds greeted her final parting. She has winged her way to heaven from the Eternal City she loved so well . . . from this "Holy City."

Father Bonaventura hurried to Via dei Baldassini and that same evening Sister Elena's brother and the members of the General Council, Sister Angelica, Sister Celina, Sister Teresa Infusino and Sister Rita arrived from Cosenza. Sister Elena's death had thoroughly shaken them.

Her mortal remains were lovingly moved to the Chapel that was banked with white flowers. The Sisters, Madame Veturia Zanelli and her daughter waked in prayer all night long. Besides the loyal ladies who had greeted her arrival, the following distinguished persons came to pay their last respects: the former Prefects of Cosenza: The Hon. Guido Palmardita and daughters and the Hon. Gaetano Marfisa: also Dr. Dario Crocetta and Dr. Giuseppe Trombetta both of the Secretariat of Hon. Colombo, and Monsignor Umberto Cameli. The Hon. Salvatore Foderaro, who was deeply affected, looked after the transfer of the coffin from Rome to Cosenza as well as for the burial permit within the Chapel of the Mother House. Father Francesco Mazza of the Minims arrived on the morning of June 20 and said Holy Mass in the Chapel with several other Priests. A Solemn Funeral Blessing took place that afternoon in the Parish Church. The chanting was rendered by the Caterinian Sisters, better known as the Sisters of the Poor on Guanella Square. Present also were quite many Sisters from several Religious Communities and all the Parish Associations as well. At 4:30 P.M., the casket was on its way to Cosenza. His Excellency, the Hon. Guido Palmardita, dispatched the following telegram to the Mother House: "As your late venerable Foundress leaves Rome from the House on Via dei Baldassini, I pray with you with the certainity that your saintly Mother will ever more enlighten, protect and direct your Congregation which, with admirable self-denial, takes care of abandoned girls. The great concourse of people and the profusion of white flowers have been a deserved tribute to your Mother General now returning to her own great and generous land, a land strong and unforgettable for virtue, for culture and for her people."

Palmardita

The casket arrived at Cosenza on June 21, shortly after 10 A.M. It had previously reached Montalto Uffugo after a brief halt at the Acri and Bisignano Cross Roads. The news had spread about and so crowds came from all sides to pay their respects and to pray. Following the eulogy by Counsellor Armando Di Napoli, the funeral car left Montalto and passed through the villages of S. Sisto dei Valdesi, Bucita and S. Fili, each one representing stepping stones of her struggles and works. The casket was taken to the Cathedral at Cosenza, where the Holy Mass was offered up in presence of all the Authorities. Father Sarago preached Sister Elena's eulogy, then Archbishop Calcara imparted the funeral blessing. Carried by the Sister Minims the coffin was again placed on the funeral car. First in line were delegations from the houses established by Sister Elena; after them came delegations of the City's Religious Institutes and of Catholic Associations. Great crowds closed the procession. In the Chapel's Institute the coffin was laid open to view and that was the beginning of a sad pilgrimage. The concourse of all classes of people continued the whole day.

CHAPTER SIXTEEN

Portrait of the Valiant Woman

We were about writing the last chapter in order to describe more vividly some of the events which had been barely mentioned here and there, when the Very Rev. Father Bonaventura da Pavullo, quite providentially, came to our aid by this masterly portrayal of our subject. No doubt our readers will appreciate his kind gesture.

"Ave Maria"
Very Rev. and dear Monsignor:

I am told that you are writing the life story of Sister Elena Aiello, Foundress of the Sister Minims of the Passion of O.L.J.C., of Cosenza, who died in odor of sanctity three years ago. You are quite able to do so because of your close and friendly association with her. For this reason I think that you, Monsignor, will be pleased to receive my personal impressions concerning the character of that Religious whom I steadily watched, greatly admired and reverently loved. I deem also to be my duty to do so because, for over 10 years, I was closely associated with her in my capacity as Religious Assistant to her Congregation—a position that I still hold.

Today, after a considerable lapse of time, the more I think of her, the greater she appears to me, ever charming, ever worthy of highest praise, though so unaffected and unskilled in human wisdom. Quite naturally St. Paul's saying comes to my mind: "The weak things of the world has God chosen, to confound the strong" . . . and now Sister Elena may well intone her "Magnificat" to God Who "has regarded the lowliness of His handmade for He Who is mighty has done great things to me!"

On my visits to that little cell of the Mother House, Via dei Martiri, No. 9, I would usually find her lying down on a white bed, to which she was confined for nearly twenty hours a day. That visit was a little feast for both of us. Our conversation lasted long because of the many subjects and affairs we had to discuss. She would willingly open her mind and speak at length concerning a hundred topics, such as the soul, or her Institute's series of joys, and sorrows, anxieties and hopes. Thereafter, she would turn her attention to the religious, political and social events of the day which she would interpret so accurately as to seem almost prophetic.

She also shared wholeheartedly the triumphs and sorrows of the Church, of the Nation, and of any individual person. She loved to speak at length about them and to offer her prayers and her mysterious sufferings to that end. I never went away from those meetings without feeling greatly edified and deeply absorbed in thought. Sister Elena was truly the valiant woman of the Holy Writ.

In spite of her limited education, for which the Calabrian women of her time didn't have much opportunity, she possessed a keen mind, a very practical intuition, a great common sense and a sturdy will that at times was wrongly interpreted as obstinacy. At such times I would teasingly exclaim: "Daughter of the Calabrian Rocks!" However, she would humbly cry out: "Please don't say that, just tell me what to do and I shall obey without saying a word." This proves how correctly she acted and how well she could control her strong character and outstanding personality, when necessary. As a rule, she would express herself in that typical Calabrian dialect—so flowing and trenchant—of her native Montalto Uffugo. She abhorred any kind of posing or duplicity. She was always childlike in her words and deeds, even when dealing with Church Authorities.

On such occasions she never failed to show them the proper respect any they in turn, far from showing any resentment or astonishment, felt very much pleased and edified. Her ardent spirit of faith, so very natural to her, was her guiding star in all her actions and enterprises. She used to speak about Jesus and Mary as one would of family members, and she ever entertained the tenderest devotion for the Blessed Eucharistic, for the Sacred Passion of Jesus and for our Sorrowful Mother, Mediatrix between man and God.

She kept the rosary beads wrapped around her wrists so as to be able to say it at any free moment of the day. She loved to keep the Church neat and beautiful, to decorate the Altar with fresh flowers and to ever foster greater solemnity and unction for the Sacred Functions. Though she had a very delicate conscience, she never permitted mechanical, formalistic piety to get the best of her.

Her way of acting toward God was just like that of her special Patroness, St. Teresa, i.e., a wonderful familiarity, complete surrender and childlike abandon. No matter how unimportant, her conversation was always distinguished by religious expressions or allusions without either effort or affection. She realized perfectly well that she was an insignificant and worthless creature, because she was truly humble according to the saying of St. Teresa of Avila "that humility is truth."

This explains why she would talk with such ease, about her mystical phenomenon with Priests and preferably with prudent and trustworthy persons. She would do so with all simplicity and ingenuity, because she only aimed to please God. Her spirit of sincerity and candor was truly enchanting. She couldn't tolerate wile or duplicity for which she had nothing but complete contempt. She would forcefully denounce and resist any kind of injustice from whatever quarters, particularly when it concerned the poor, the weak and the defenseless.

Many a time she sacrificed human prudence and social standards in order to voice her indignation against exploiters, and threatened them with God's severe punishments as well as with the condemnation of honest people. Naturally she met with misunderstanding, humiliations and even material loss on account of her frank and intrepid conduct. In spite of all, she never backed down and never played dumb.

A truly valiant and strong woman, frail in body but of the Baptist and the Catherine type, all the more worthy of praise and admiration at a time when the spirit of servility was in vogue. Feeling conscious of her freedom as a child of God, she would not hesitate to address the mighty ones, even the very Chiefs of State and the Nations' Rulers with utmost frankness albeit always in a respectful way.

The only thing she really dreaded and abhorred was the evil of sin, against which she ever fought wherever she found it. On the other hand she felt motherly compassion for sinners, and for their salvation she never spared prayers, tears or pains. In a world that is today engrossed with crass materialism, Sister Elena lifted high the banner of lily-white purity, and insisted both with her Sisters and with those dwelling in her houses to keep it spotless, at all cost, through the blessing of Divine Grace and the protection of the Blessed Virgin.

In that respect she was quite exemplary because her enchanting reserve and her purity seemed to spread a heavenly fragance. She loved to say that what the world needs today is a threefold profession of humility, charity and purity. Those who were well acquainted with her could bear witness to the humble opinion she had of herself and of the work she was carrying out. She preferred to act rather than talk. On being requested to open new houses of her Congregation both in Northern Italy and in America, she invariably replied: "We are not in a position to do so, because the Sisters there are supposed to be very capable and well trained." This way of speaking was due to her great humility, because, as a matter of fact, her Sisters were very well trained indeed, and could have given a good account of themselves anywhere else.

Since the love of neighbor is a true reflection of our love for God, Sister Elena resolved to give her life and her work without stint to fulfill that mission. She supported equally well all works of mercy both spiritual and temporal, and always gave them preferential consideration. Above all she was a truly loving Mother to her little ones and found happiness in all the sacrifices, worries and responsibilities inherent to that work. She went out of her way doing good to those who were feeble or sick, for in them she beheld Jesus, the Good Shepherd Whom she tried to imitate to the best of her ability.

She was all aflame and waxed eloquent whenever she had occasion to speak about the several houses of her Congregation and the manifold activities held therein. More than once I heard her saying: "Should anyone ever dare to lay hands on my works I shall rise from my grave in their defense." She spared neither hardship nor any sacrifices when it was a question of making her work produce better results and a greater amount of good. Whenever the occasion required it, she would set aside her natural reserve, and either write to, or call upon, important people. In addition she would organize exhibitions of articles made by her orphan girls, and prepare shows, recitals etc., etc.

How true indeed that love conquers all! All her Houses were attuned to the magic word "Charitas" which was the basic program of her Institution. Sisters and Orphans were treated alike. Their sorrows and joys were shared in common, because they were all children of the same Father, Who is in heaven. All the benefactors of her Houses experienced the delicate attention of her noble and grateful soul. She appreciated saintly friendships and she was true to them in time of need and at the time of death. Very few persons could equal her for hard work. As long as she was able to be on her feet, she was always the first to rise and the last to retire. She used to take up the most humble chores, nay she would reserve for herself the hardest and the most boring ones. Furthermore, she was a tireless worker. Even when bedridden she would shun idleness, which she considered as her capital enemy.

At such a time she either knitted or checked the Sisters' and Orphans' work, because among other things she was an expert in embroidery and in cut-work. She also gave spiritual instructions to Novices and Postulants, took care of her heavy mail, would study problems and give decisions on legal and administrative matters and projects of her many Houses after consultation with competent people. Her room had an appearance of a quartermaster's office filled with papers and pamphlets that were strewn even on her bed. Though having limited instruction, yet because of her keen mind and long experience, she had become highly competent in the solution of even the most intricate problems.

Worth mentioning is the fact that in her Houses, even during working hours, the Holy Rosary and other prayers were frequently said and everybody was reminded of the presence of God, to Whom every action was directed and for Whom everything was done. Whatever Sister Elena was preaching, she would always be the very first to practice. Finally we should point out her great love and profound veneration for the Church and for our Holy Father, the Pope. Whenever she mentioned his name she felt deeply moved, and she would have willingly given up her life for the Pope "the gentle Christ on earth" and for the Church. On occasion of some solemn celebrations she wanted hymns to be sung in his honor and his picture to be publicly displayed. Nothing would pain her so much as when she would hear that the Church and its visible Head were being reviled. Then oh, how promptly she would rise to their defense! She appeared to have the courage of a lion in her eagerness to defeat the Pope's enemies! Better still, she desired that all the faithful should give witness to the holiness of their

Mother the Church more by their deeds than by their words.

Someone remarked that she had not been as submissive to the Clergy in general as she had been to the Supreme Authority of the Church. But evidently whoever spoke that way did not really know Sister Elena. For she did love and esteem very much the whole Hierarchy of the Church, and the undersigned can submit any amount of proofs to that end. But just because of that great love and appreciation, she did sometimes censure some of the acts that did not reflect honor on the clerical state.

On the other hand she willingly suffered and prayed with her whole heart so that Religious and Priests might become like their spouse, the Church, without spot or wrinkle. How often during her conversation she would fervently urge me to do all in my power to foster vocations for the Sanctuary and Altar, i.e., for good Priests and still more saintly Priests who would be the light and the salt of the earth!

Her little cell was a frequent pilgrimage for Priests, Religious and even Bishops. Sister Elena was always most happy to welcome them because she beheld in them the very Person of Jesus Christ Who is ever present in saintly Priests and in souls consecrated to Him.

FATHER BONAVENTURA DA PAVULLO
Def. Gen. Cap.
Pontifical Assistant to the Sister Minims of the Passion of O.L.J.C.

Rome, May 13, 1964

CHAPTER SEVENTEEN

Is Hysteria the Last Word?

DR. ADOLFO TURANO wrote as follows, concerning the phenomena, as they occurred the first time.

"On the First Friday of March 1923, about 3 P.M., I was called to the home of Elena Aiello. I found her lying down, her head leaning to one side, and the eyes half-open. Blood was oozing out of her forehead, streaming down on face and neck and utterly drenching her pillowcase. The very abandon of her arms, the lines on her face, so expressive of profound sadness, her head bowed down and turned to one side, her lips and eyes barely open, made her stand out as a picture of the true mystic.

Now and then she would take up a rigid posture, lift up her head, intently focus her wide-open eyes upon some invisible object and register various expressions on her face. By just looking at her, one could easily guess her emotions either of anguish and terror or of happiness and heavenly contemplation.

When her face muscles contracted, blood would trickle down through the skin. Her bleeding was more abundant at the center of her forehead, but tiny drops of blood were also running down from her head. The moment the ecstasy was over, the patient, in a low but distinct tone of voice, would recount how she had seen Jesus bleeding on the Cross. In their excitement over that singular and amazing phenomenon, all the members of her family, her Confessor, relatives and friends, quickly assembled in her bedroom, where, to their surprise, Elena questioned them whether they also had witnessed the Divine Tragedy. That phenomenon lasted three hours during which time the bleeding occurred now and then and the patient reflected some unusual features on her face.

Thereafter Elena was her old self again, and, though thoroughly worn out, she recovered very quickly so that, the following day she was up early and promptly resumed her usual duties.

Counsellor Di Napoli, who was an eye-witness to the Good Friday phenomenon in 1924, described it in this way. "On that day Dr. Fabrizio, a Professor at the University of Naples and a man of ocnsiderable culture, came to visit bedridden Elena Aiello, popularly known as the "holy Nun." He had been invited by Dr. A. Turano, the family physician and a fine professional man.

About Springtime, Dr. Turano sought to induce Master Pasquale to consent to his daughter's transfer to Dr. Fabrizio's clinic for medical observation and for checking the truth about the reality of the phenomenon on the previous year. Master Pasquale firmly refused because he jealously guarded his children whom he had brought up with loving and diligent care. However, later on, owing to Dr. Turano's insistance, he permitted Dr. Fabrizio to visit Elena at home. The phenomenon took place regularly during the Fridays in Lent.

To offset the people's curiosity, Elena, in one of her frequent visions, beseeched Jesus to remove the stigmata from her hands. Jesus was pleased to grant her request by the substitution of additional inward pain.

At the first manifestation of the phenomena on Friday, Dean Mauro who was anxious to verify whether they were caused by religious obsession or by some form of hysteria, decided to test Elena's good faith. On the third Friday Elena asked her sister Emma to accompany her to the dining room, but exactly at 3 P.M., she started feeling unbearable pain. Wishing to relieve her suffering, the patient and desolate Emma coaxed her to go to bed, but Elena refused saying that she had been "ordered to resist." However, after a while she had to give in owing to the persistent pain. She had taken but a few steps when suddenly she was seized by convulsions, and, dropping down to the floor, she was badly hurt for quite sometime.

On Good Friday in 1924, besides the bleeding on her forehead, she was also marked with stigmata on her feet and with some bruises on her knees. I was a witness to that phenomenon from beginning to end. Since an enormous crowd had assembled, the carabineers found it hard to hold back so many people who had come from nearby villages and from other localities. For they were most anxious to find out what was going on and they were deeply moved when they saw bedridden Elena convulsed with agonizing pain. Groups of pilgrims were constantly on the move, up and down stairs, and they were either whispering to one another or were simply abosrbed in silent meditation. The members of her family, the relatives and friends had gathered in one large room and they looked very much surprised at the large attendance of strangers. And all the while no one paid any attention to the dangerous condition of the floor which was supporting a weight much superior to its load.

When photographer Serra and I arrived, Elena was already in ecstatic contemplation. She seemed to be extremely happy while intently looking at some invisible object. Previous to the bleeding, Elena had been lamenting from time to time, as if being tortured, but once the blood started trickling down from her forehead all over her face, she cried out several times: "How light is this crown of thorns on my head! How small, O my God, is this torture compared to Yours!"

At times she was restless: for a while she would lay exhausted: if the bleeding stopped for a moment or so, it would shortly start all over again. On April 18, 1924, about 10:30 A.M., the Procession of the Mysteries had left the little Church of San Giacomo, on City Hall Square, to wind its way through the streets of that town. That date had been carefully checked in order to verify a statement made by Elena's people that the phenomenon was due to happen at the very beginning of the Procession as on the previous year.

Professor Fabrizio came in together with Dr. Turano about 11 A.M., when the phenomenon had already started. Elena's laments were being interspersed with brief moments of ecstasy. Dr. Matteo Caracciolo and Dr. Alfredo Scotti, the town's official physicians, the Mayor, Chev. Giuseppe Paglilla, Counsellor Marc. Giorgio Alimena and friends looked around for a little while and went their way. A press reporter also came in for a moment or so, and left in search for news.

Since Prof. Fabrizio was highly thought of, his ruling that no one should be admitted to the patient's room, outside of Dr. Turano, himself, photographer Serra and myself, was strictly observed. When Elena regained temporary consciousness, she showed displeasure at seeing four unwelcome guests in her room. Approaching her, Dr. Turano sought to calm her by saying: "Elena dear, I am you 'compare' Adolfo Turano. You know I wouldn't hurt you." Meanwhile, Dr. Fabrizio seeing that the blood was flowing in larger quantity, started gathering some of it on tiny panels of glass. Each time he happened to pass the glass over the forehead on the spot whence the blood was flowing, Elena screamed wildly because of the unbearable pain. Photographer Serra was completely puzzled, for no matter how he tried, he couldn't get his camera to click.

Before trying any other experiment, Prof. Fabrizio wished to take a look at the stigmata on Elena's feet and at the bruises on her knees. So Dr. Turano lifted up the patient's right foot high enough to allow Dr. Fabrizio to insert two small tapers through the lower and upper part of the stigmata. That operation caused such excruciating pain to poor Elena that her people, rushing into the room, demanded to put a stop to such cruelty. Hence, it was no longer possible to proceed with the examination of her body, except a short observation of the bruises on the knees, of the arms and of the upper part of her breast.

Dr. Turano and Dr. Fabrizio concluded their medical examination by saying that this strange case of phenomenology should be relegated to the field of hysteria. But, Dr. Matteo Caracciolo, who was not exactly the type of a pious man, was more realistic, when, with characteristic common sense, he ventured to say: "As far as I am concerned, I see that in this case we are face to face with the supernatural."

Let us now take a look at the report submitted by Chev. Dr. G. Battista Molezzi to His Excellency Roberto Nogara, Archbishop of Cosenza on November 23, 1938.

"What I am goin to write concerning Sister Elena Aiello, in whose body some amazing phenomena take place on Good

Friday, is the result of my personal experience both at her home at Montalto Uffugo and in her Institute, "The Little Abandoned Girls" at Cosenza. I shall not deal with useless questions, neither shall I discuss religious matters. I shall simply report what I myself saw and felt on those Fridays. To be sure I was profoundly stirred on those days by the spectacle of the bleeding stigmata and by the awesome sight of that poor body convulsed with terrific pain.

I shall not mention the few cases when Elena recovered instantly from serious illness without human remedies, but solely through direct supernatural intervention, as she herself admitted. Some day, if God grants me the grace and the strength to do so, I shall deal with them at length in a book that I hope to write on the life of this stigmatic Nun.

Before going any further we should take into account the physical condition of Sister Elena. She consumes but a frugal meal consisting of some vegetables and water, yet she goes about filling her schedule of manifold duties that would break the fiber of even a robust constitution. And she does all this in spite of her continuous suffering.

Insdeed, it may be said of her that she lives by her daily fast which, though not as spectacular as is the case with stigmatic Theresa Neumann, it is quite remarkable just the same. Worth remembering too is the fact that the bleeding on her stigmata occurs on Good Friday, at exactly the same hour as Jesus suffered on the Cross. Blood keeps oozing out of her forehead, apparently punctured by sharp thorns, from her side, her hands and her feet. On one occasion when Doctors pushed splinters through the wounds on her feet, we got the distinct impression that these had been pierced by actual nails.

The bleeding of the stigmata is so abundant as to utterly drench a lot of linen. Once the phenomenon is over, Elena reposes in a comatose stage, which is frequently interrupted by some painful visions. She stretches out her arms and keeps her eyes wide-open as if struck by a dreadful scene. On regaining consciousness she tells the story of having witnessed the Passion of Our Lord and of having partaken to that Divine Tragedy. After Good Friday all phenomena disappear at once. All that is left on her side, on her hands and feet, is some sort of a pink crust which stays on for good.

It is also an extraordinary fact that Sister Elena, though so worn out, as if her very life were coming to an end, yet on Holy Saturday morning rises cheerful and strong as ever, just as if nothing unusual had happened to her on the previous day.

Several attempts have been made to explain these phenomena on grounds of hysteria or of some impaired nervous system. But in all fairness I think that we should ask ourselves this simple question: "Is it because of our ignorance that we are unable to explain a biological and pathological case of phenomenology? Or is it rather because we are in presence of a mystery, which is elusive to human science?"

When all is said and done, this much is certain, i.e., that after viewing that poor body tortured by indescribable pain, as you leave that room, you cannot possibly forget that face smeared with blood flowing from forehead and both temples. It is not possible to forget the vision of that body agonizing with pain at the slightest touch on its wounds.

Ordinary people and learned men stand by perplexed and perturbed, no knowing what to say or what to do. But fair-minded persons willingly admit that there must be some unknown and hidden power that shows the way how to solve the doubt by simply acknowledging that we are in presence of a mystery.

Otherwise it would be humanly impossible that this soul, consumed with love, could supply strength to a body tortured by pain, unless it were supported by a Supreme Being.

This is what in my capacity, as the family physician, I can conscientiously attest concerning the life of Sister Elena Aiello.

